NON SANZ DROICT.

William Shakespeare

ALL'S WELL
THAT ENDS WELL

Edited by Sylvan Barnet

The Signet Classic Shakespeare
GENERAL EDITOR: SYLVAN BARNET

Revised and Updated
Bibliography

A SIGNET CLASSIC
NEW AMERICAN LIBRARY
TIMES MIRROR
NEW YORK AND SCARBOROUGH, ONTARIO

First Signet Printing, June, 1965

SIGNET CLASSIC TRADEMARK REG. U.S. PAT. OFF. AND FOREIGN COUNTRIES
REGISTERED TRADEMARK—MARCA REGISTRADA
HECHO EN CHICAGO, U.S.A.

SIGNET, SIGNET CLASSICS, MENTOR, PLUME, MERIDIAN AND NAL
BOOKS *are published in the United States by*
The New American Library of World Literature, Inc.,
1633 Broadway, New York, New York 10019,
in Canada by The New American Library of Canada Limited,
81 Mack Avenue, Scarborough, Ontario M1L 1M8

5   6   7   8   9   10   11   12

PRINTED IN THE UNITED STATES OF AMERICA

Contents

SHAKESPEARE: PREFATORY REMARKS   *vii*

INTRODUCTION   *xxi*

All's Well That Ends Well   43

TEXTUAL NOTE   159

THE SOURCE OF *All's Well That Ends Well*   163

    William Painter: from *The Palace of Pleasure*   165

COMMENTARIES   175

    Samuel Johnson: from *The Plays of William Shakespeare*   175

    M. C. Bradbrook: from *Shakespeare and Elizabethan Poetry*   177

    Richard David: from *Plays Pleasant and Plays Unpleasant*   189

SUGGESTED REFERENCES   195

Shakespeare: Prefatory Remarks

Between the record of his baptism in Stratford on 26 April 1564 and the record of his burial in Stratford on 25 April 1616, some forty documents name Shakespeare, and many others name his parents, his children, and his grandchildren. More facts are known about William Shakespeare than about any other playwright of the period except Ben Jonson. The facts should, however, be distinguished from the legends. The latter, inevitably more engaging and better known, tell us that the Stratford boy killed a calf in high style, poached deer and rabbits, and was forced to flee to London, where he held horses outside a playhouse. These traditions are only traditions; they may be true, but no evidence supports them, and it is well to stick to the facts.

Mary Arden, the dramatist's mother, was the daughter of a substantial landowner; about 1557 she married John Shakespeare, who was a glove-maker and trader in various farm commodities. In 1557 John Shakespeare was a member of the Council (the governing body of Stratford), in 1558 a constable of the borough, in 1561 one of the two town chamberlains, in 1565 an alderman (entitling him to the appellation "Mr."), in 1568 high bailiff—the town's highest political office, equivalent to mayor. After 1577, for an unknown reason he drops out of local politics. The birthday of William Shakespeare, the eldest son of this locally prominent man, is unrecorded; but the Stratford parish register records that the infant was baptized on 26 April 1564. (It is quite possible that he was born on 23 April, but this date has probably been assigned by tradition because it is the date on which, fifty-two years later, he died.) The attendance records of the Stratford grammar school of the period are not extant, but it is reasonable to assume that the son of a local official attended the school and received substantial training in Latin. The masters of the school from Shakespeare's seventh to fifteenth years held Oxford degrees; the Elizabethan curriculum excluded mathematics and the natural sciences but taught a good deal of Latin rhetoric, logic, and literature. On 27 November 1582 a marriage license was issued to Shakespeare and Anne Hathaway, eight years his senior. The couple had a child in May, 1583. Perhaps the marriage was necessary, but perhaps the couple had earlier engaged in a formal "troth plight" which would render their children legitimate even if no further ceremony were performed. In 1585 Anne Hathaway bore Shakespeare twins.

That Shakespeare was born is excellent; that he married and had children is pleasant; but that we know nothing about his departure from Stratford to London, or about the beginning of his theatrical career, is lamentable and must be admitted. We would gladly sacrifice details about his children's baptism for details about his earliest days on the stage. Perhaps the poaching episode is true (but it is first reported almost a century after Shakespeare's death), or perhaps he first left Stratford to be a schoolteacher, as another tradition holds; perhaps he was moved by

> Such wind as scatters young men through the world,
> To seek their fortunes further than at home
> Where small experience grows.

In 1592, thanks to the cantankerousness of Robert Greene, a rival playwright and a pamphleteer, we have our first reference, a snarling one, to Shakespeare as an actor and playwright. Greene warns those of his own educated friends who wrote for the theater against an actor who has presumed to turn playwright:

> There is an upstart crow, beautified with our feathers, that with his *tiger's heart wrapped in a player's hide* supposes he is as well able to bombast out a blank verse

as the best of you, and being an absolute Johannes-
factotum is in his own conceit the only Shake-scene in
a country.

The reference to the player, as well as the allusion to
Aesop's crow (who strutted in borrowed plumage, as an
actor struts in fine words not his own), makes it clear that
by this date Shakespeare had both acted and written. That
Shakespeare is meant is indicated not only by "Shake-scene"
but by the parody of a line from one of Shakespeare's plays,
3 Henry VI: "O, tiger's heart wrapped in a woman's hide."
If Shakespeare in 1592 was prominent enough to be at-
tacked by an envious dramatist, he probably had served an
apprenticeship in the theater for at least a few years.

In any case, by 1592 Shakespeare had acted and written,
and there are a number of subsequent references to him as
an actor: documents indicate that in 1598 he is a "principal
comedian," in 1603 a "principal tragedian," in 1608 he is
one of the "men players." The profession of actor was not
for a gentleman, and it occasionally drew the scorn of
university men who resented writing speeches for persons
less educated than themselves, but it was respectable
enough: players, if prosperous, were in effect members of
the bourgeoisie, and there is nothing to suggest that Stratford considered William Shakespeare less than a solid citizen. When, in 1596, the Shakespeares were granted a coat
of arms, the grant was made to Shakespeare's father, but
probably William Shakespeare (who the next year bought
the second-largest house in town) had arranged the matter
on his own behalf. In subsequent transactions he is occasionally styled a gentleman.

Although in 1593 and 1594 Shakespeare published two
narrative poems dedicated to the Earl of Southampton,
Venus and Adonis and *The Rape of Lucrece,* and may well
have written most or all of his sonnets in the middle nineties,
Shakespeare's literary activity seems to have been almost
entirely devoted to the theater. (It may be significant that
the two narrative poems were written in years when the
plague closed the theaters for several months.) In 1594
he was a charter member of a theatrical company called the

Chamberlain's Men (which in 1603 changed its name to the King's Men); until he retired to Stratford (about 1611, apparently), he was with this remarkably stable company. From 1599 the company acted primarily at the Globe Theatre, in which Shakespeare held a one-tenth interest. Other Elizabethan dramatists are known to have acted, but no other is known also to have been entitled to a share in the profits of the playhouse.

Shakespeare's first eight published plays did not have his name on them, but this is not remarkable; the most popular play of the sixteenth century, Thomas Kyd's *The Spanish Tragedy,* went through many editions without naming Kyd, and Kyd's authorship is known only because a book on the profession of acting happens to quote (and attribute to Kyd) some lines on the interest of Roman emperors in the drama. What is remarkable is that after 1598 Shakespeare's name commonly appears on printed plays—some of which are not his. Another indication of his popularity comes from Francis Meres, author of *Palladis Tamia: Wit's Treasury* (1598): in this anthology of snippets accompanied by an essay on literature, many playwrights are mentioned, but Shakespeare's name occurs more often than any other, and Shakespeare is the only playwright whose plays are listed.

From his acting, playwriting, and share in a theater, Shakespeare seems to have made considerable money. He put it to work, making substantial investments in Stratford real estate. When he made his will (less than a month before he died), he sought to leave his property intact to his descendants. Of small bequests to relatives and to friends (including three actors, Richard Burbage, John Heminges, and Henry Condell), that to his wife of the second-best bed has provoked the most comment; perhaps it was the bed the couple had slept in, the best being reserved for visitors. In any case, had Shakespeare not excepted it, the bed would have gone (with the rest of his household possessions) to his daughter and her husband. On 25 April 1616 he was buried within the chancel of the church at Stratford. An unattractive monument to his memory, placed on a wall near the grave, says he died on 23 April. Over the grave itself are the lines, perhaps by Shakespeare, that (more than his literary fame) have kept his bones undisturbed in the crowded burial ground where old bones were often dislodged to make way for new:

> Good friend, for Jesus' sake forbear
> To dig the dust enclosèd here.
> Blessed be the man that spares these stones
> And cursed be he that moves my bones.

Thirty-seven plays, as well as some nondramatic poems, are held to constitute the Shakespeare canon. The dates of composition of most of the works are highly uncertain, but there is often.evidence of a *terminus a quo* (starting point) and/or a *terminus ad quem* (terminal point) that provides a framework for intelligent guessing. For example, *Richard II* cannot be earlier than 1595, the publication date of some material to which it is indebted; *The Merchant of Venice* cannot be later than 1598, the year Francis Meres mentioned it. Sometimes arguments for a date hang on an alleged topical allusion, such as the lines about the unseasonable weather in *A Midsummer Night's Dream,* II.i.81–117, but such an allusion (if indeed it is an allusion) can be variously interpreted, and in any case there is always the possibility that a topical allusion was inserted during a revision, years after the composition of a play. Dates are often attributed on the basis of style, and although conjectures about style usually rest on other conjectures, sooner or later one must rely on one's literary sense. There is no real proof, for example, that *Othello* is not as early as *Romeo and Juliet,* but one feels *Othello* is later, and because the first record of its performance is 1604, one is glad enough to set its composition at that date and not push it back into Shakespeare's early years. The following chronology, then, is as much indebted to informed guesswork and sensitivity as it is to fact. The dates, necessarily imprecise, indicate something like a scholarly consensus.

PLAYS

1588–93	*The Comedy of Errors*
1588–94	*Love's Labor's Lost*

1590–91	*2 Henry VI*
1590–91	*3 Henry VI*
1591–92	*1 Henry VI*
1592–93	*Richard III*
1592–94	*Titus Andronicus*
1593–94	*The Taming of the Shrew*
1593–95	*The Two Gentlemen of Verona*
1594–96	*Romeo and Juliet*
1595	*Richard II*
1594–96	*A Midsummer Night's Dream*
1596–97	*King John*
1596–97	*The Merchant of Venice*
1597	*1 Henry IV*
1597–98	*2 Henry IV*
1598–1600	*Much Ado About Nothing*
1598–99	*Henry V*
1599	*Julius Caesar*
1599–1600	*As You Like It*
1599–1600	*Twelfth Night*
1600–01	*Hamlet*
1597–1601	*The Merry Wives of Windsor*
1601–02	*Troilus and Cressida*
1602–04	*All's Well That Ends Well*
1603–04	*Othello*
1604	*Measure for Measure*
1605–06	*King Lear*
1605–06	*Macbeth*
1606–07	*Antony and Cleopatra*
1605–08	*Timon of Athens*
1607–09	*Coriolanus*
1608	*Pericles*
1609–10	*Cymbeline*
1610–11	*The Winter's Tale*
1611	*The Tempest*
1612–13	*Henry VIII*

POEMS

| 1592 | *Venus and Adonis* |
| 1593–94 | *The Rape of Lucrece* |

1593–1600   *Sonnets*
1600–01   *The Phoenix and Turtle*

Shakespeare's Theater

In Shakespeare's infancy, Elizabethan actors performed wherever they could—in great halls, at court, in the court-yards of inns. The innyards must have made rather unsatis-factory theaters: on some days they were unavailable be-cause carters bringing goods to London used them as depots; when available, they had to be rented from the innkeeper; perhaps most important, London inns were sub-ject to the Common Council of London, which was not well disposed toward theatricals. In 1574 the Common Coun-cil required that plays and playing places in London be licensed. It asserted that

> sundry great disorders and inconveniences have been found to ensue to this city by the inordinate haunting of great multitudes of people, specially youth, to plays, interludes, and shows, namely occasion of frays and quarrels, evil practices of incontinency in great inns having chambers and secret places adjoining to their open stages and galleries,

and ordered that innkeepers who wished licenses to hold performances put up a bond and make contributions to the poor.

The requirement that plays and innyard theaters be licensed, along with the other drawbacks of playing at inns, probably drove James Burbage (a carpenter-turned-actor) to rent in 1576 a plot of land northeast of the city walls and to build here—on property outside the jurisdiction of the city—England's first permanent construction designed for plays. He called it simply the Theatre. About all that is known of its construction is that it was wood. It soon had imitators, the most famous being the Globe (1599), built across the Thames (again outside the city's jurisdiction), out of timbers of the Theatre, which had been dismantled when Burbage's lease ran out.

There are three important sources of information about the structure of Elizabethan playhouses—drawings, a contract, and stage directions in plays. Of drawings, only the so-called De Witt drawing (c. 1596) of the Swan—really a friend's copy of De Witt's drawing—is of much significance. It shows a building of three tiers, with a stage jutting from a wall into the yard or center of the building. The tiers are roofed, and part of the stage is covered by a roof that projects from the rear and is supported at its front on two posts, but the groundlings, who paid a penny to stand in front of the stage, were exposed to the sky. (Performances in such a playhouse were held only in the daytime; artificial illumination was not used.) At the rear of the stage are two doors; above the stage is a gallery. The second major source of information, the contract for the Fortune, specifies that although the Globe is to be the model, the Fortune is to be square, eighty feet outside and fifty-five inside. The stage is to be forty-three feet broad, and is to extend into the middle of the yard (i.e., it is twenty-seven and a half feet deep). For patrons willing to pay more than the general admission charged of the groundlings, there were to be three galleries provided with seats. From the third chief source, stage directions, one learns that entrance to the stage was by doors, presumably spaced widely apart at the rear ("Enter one citizen at one door, and another at the other"), and that in addition to the platform stage there was occasionally some sort of curtained booth or alcove allowing for "discovery" scenes, and some sort of playing space "aloft" or "above" to represent (for example) the top of a city's walls or a room above the street. Doubtless each theater had its own peculiarities, but perhaps we can talk about a "typical" Elizabethan theater if we realize that no theater need exactly have fit the description, just as no father is the typical father with 3.7 children. This hypothetical theater is wooden, round or polygonal (in *Henry V* Shakespeare calls it a "wooden *O*"), capable of holding some eight hundred spectators standing in the yard around the projecting elevated stage and some fifteen hundred additional spectators seated in the three roofed galleries. The stage, protected by a "shadow" or "heavens" or roof, is entered by two doors; behind the doors is the "tiring house" (attiring house, i.e., dressing room), and above the doors is some sort of gallery that may sometimes hold spectators but that can be used (for example) as the bedroom from which Romeo—according to a stage direction in one text—"goeth down." Some evidence suggests that a throne can be lowered onto the platform stage, perhaps from the "shadow"; certainly characters can descend from the stage through a trap or traps into the cellar or "hell." Sometimes this space beneath the platform accommodates a sound-effects man or musician (in *Antony and Cleopatra* "music of the hautboys is under the stage") or an actor (in *Hamlet* the "Ghost cries under the stage"). Most characters simply walk on and off, but because there is no curtain in front of the platform, corpses will have to be carried off (Hamlet must lug Polonius' guts into the neighbor room), or will have to fall at the rear, where the curtain on the alcove or booth can be drawn to conceal them.

Such may have been the so-called "public theater." Another kind of theater, called the "private theater" because its much greater admission charge limited its audience to the wealthy or the prodigal, must be briefly mentioned. The private theater was basically a large room, entirely roofed and therefore artificially illuminated, with a stage at one end. In 1576 one such theater was established in Blackfriars, a Dominican priory in London that had been suppressed in 1538 and confiscated by the Crown and thus was not under the city's jurisdiction. All the actors in the Blackfriars theater were boys about eight to thirteen years old (in the public theaters similar boys played female parts; a boy Lady Macbeth played to a man Macbeth). This private theater had a precarious existence, and ceased operations in 1584. In 1596 James Burbage, who had already made theatrical history by building the Theatre, began to construct a second Blackfriars theater. He died in 1597, and for several years this second Blackfriars theater was used by a troupe of boys, but in 1608 two of Burbage's sons and five other actors (including Shakespeare) became joint operators of the theater, using it in the winter when the open-air Globe was unsuitable. Perhaps such a smaller theater, roofed, artificially illuminated, and with a tradition of a courtly audience, exerted an influence on Shakespeare's late plays.

Performances in the private theaters may well have had intermissions during which music was played, but in the public theaters the action was probably uninterrupted, flowing from scene to scene almost without a break. Actors would enter, speak, exit, and others would immediately enter and establish (if necessary) the new locale by a few properties and by words and gestures. Here are some samples of Shakespeare's scene painting:

> This is Illyria, lady.

> Well, this is the Forest of Arden.

> This castle hath a pleasant seat; the air
> Nimbly and sweetly recommends itself
> Unto our gentle senses.

On the other hand, it is a mistake to conceive of the Elizabethan stage as bare. Although Shakespeare's Chorus in *Henry V* calls the stage an "unworthy scaffold" and urges the spectators to "eke out our performance with your mind," there was considerable spectacle. The last act of *Macbeth*, for example, has five stage directions calling for "drum and colors," and another sort of appeal to the eye is indicated by the stage direction "Enter Macduff, with Macbeth's head." Some scenery and properties may have been substantial; doubtless a throne was used, and in one play of the period we encounter this direction: "Hector takes up a great piece of rock and casts at Ajax, who tears up a young tree by the roots and assails Hector." The matter is of some importance, and will be glanced at again in the next section.

The Texts of Shakespeare

Though eighteen of his plays were published during his lifetime, Shakespeare seems never to have supervised their publication. There is nothing unusual here; when a play-wright sold a play to a theatrical company he surrendered his ownership of it. Normally a company would not publish the play, because to publish it meant to allow competitors to acquire the piece. Some plays, however, did get published: apparently treacherous actors sometimes pieced together a play for a publisher, sometimes a company in need of money sold a play, and sometimes a company allowed a play to be published that no longer drew audiences. That Shakespeare did not concern himself with publication, then, is scarcely remarkable; of his contemporaries only Ben Jonson carefully supervised the publication of his own plays. In 1623, seven years after Shakespeare's death, John Heminges and Henry Condell (two senior members of Shakespeare's company, who had performed with him for about twenty years) collected his plays—published and un-published—into a large volume, commonly called the First Folio. (A folio is a volume consisting of sheets that have been folded once, each sheet thus making two leaves, or four pages. The eighteen plays published during Shake-speare's lifetime had been issued one play per volume in small books called quartos. Each sheet in a quarto has been folded twice, making four leaves, or eight pages.) The First Folio contains thirty-six plays; a thirty-seventh, *Pericles,* though not in the Folio, is regarded as canonical. Heminges and Condell suggest in an address "To the great variety of readers" that the republished plays are presented in better form than in the quartos: "Before you were abused with diverse stolen and surreptitious copies, maimed and de-formed by the frauds and stealths of injurious impostors that exposed them; even those, are now offered to your view cured and perfect of their limbs, and all the rest absolute in their numbers, as he [i.e., Shakespeare] con-ceived them."

Whoever was assigned to prepare the texts for publication in the First Folio seems to have taken his job seriously and yet not to have performed it with uniform care. The sources of the texts seem to have been, in general, good unpublished copies or the best published copies. The first play in the collection, *The Tempest,* is divided into acts and scenes, has unusually full stage directions and descriptions of spectacle, and concludes with a list of the characters, but the editor was not able (or willing) to present all of the succeeding texts so fully dressed. Later texts occasionally show signs of carelessness: in one scene of *Much Ado About Nothing* the names of actors, instead of characters, appear as speech prefixes, as they had in the quarto, which the Folio reprints; proofreading throughout the Folio is spotty and apparently was done without reference to the printer's copy; the pagination of *Hamlet* jumps from 156 to 257.

A modern editor of Shakespeare must first select his copy; no problem if the play exists only in the Folio, but a considerable problem if the relationship between a quarto and the Folio—or an early quarto and a later one—is unclear. When an editor has chosen what seems to him to be the most authoritative text or texts for his copy, he has not done with making decisions. First of all, he must reckon with Elizabethan spelling. If he is not producing a facsimile, he probably modernizes it, but ought he to preserve the old form of words that apparently were pronounced quite unlike their modern forms—"lanthorn," "alablaster"? If he preserves these forms, is he really preserving Shakespeare's forms or perhaps those of a compositor in the printing house? What is one to do when one finds "lanthorn" and "lantern" in adjacent lines? (The editors of this series in general, but not invariably, assume that words should be spelled in their modern form.) Elizabethan punctuation, too, presents problems. For example in the First Folio, the only text for the play, Macbeth rejects his wife's idea that he can wash the blood from his hand:

> no: this my Hand will rather
> The multitudinous Seas incarnardine,
> Making the Greene one, Red.

Obviously an editor will remove the superfluous capitals, and he will probably alter the spelling to "incarnadine," but will he leave the comma before "red," letting Macbeth speak of the sea as "the green one," or will he (like most modern editors) remove the comma and thus have Macbeth say that his hand will make the ocean *uniformly* red?

An editor will sometimes have to change more than spelling or punctuation. Macbeth says to his wife:

> I dare do all that may become a man,
> Who dares no more, is none.

For two centuries editors have agreed that the second line is unsatisfactory, and have emended "no" to "do": "Who dares do more is none." But when in the same play Ross says that fearful persons

> floate vpon a wilde and violent Sea
> Each way, and moue,

need "move" be emended to "none," as it often is, on the hunch that the compositor misread the manuscript? The editors of the Signet Classic Shakespeare have restrained themselves from making abundant emendations. In their minds they hear Dr. Johnson on the dangers of emending: "I have adopted the Roman sentiment, that it is more honorable to save a citizen than to kill an enemy." Some departures (in addition to spelling, punctuation, and lineation) from the copy text have of course been made, but the original readings are listed in a note following the play, so that the reader can evaluate them for himself.

The editors of the Signet Classic Shakespeare, following tradition, have added line numbers and in many cases act and scene divisions as well as indications of locale at the beginning of scenes. The Folio divided most of the plays into acts and some into scenes. Early eighteenth-century editors increased the divisions. These divisions, which provide a convenient way of referring to passages in the plays, have been retained, but when not in the text chosen as the basis for the Signet Classic text they are enclosed in square brackets [ ] to indicate that they are editorial additions. Similarly, although no play of Shakespeare's published during his lifetime was equipped with indications of locale at the heads of scene divisions, locales have here been added in square brackets for the convenience of the reader, who lacks the information afforded to spectators by costumes, properties, and gestures. The spectator can tell at a glance he is in the throne room, but without an editorial indication the reader may be puzzled for a while. It should be mentioned, incidentally, that there are a few authentic stage directions—perhaps Shakespeare's, perhaps a prompter's—that suggest locales: for example, "Enter Brutus in his orchard," and "They go up into the Senate house." It is hoped that the bracketed additions provide the reader with the sort of help provided in these two authentic directions, but it is equally hoped that the reader will remember that the stage was not loaded with scenery.

No editor during the course of his work can fail to recollect some words Heminges and Condell prefixed to the Folio:

> It had been a thing, we confess, worthy to have been wished, that the author himself had lived to have set forth and overseen his own writings. But since it hath been ordained otherwise, and he by death departed from that right, we pray you do not envy his friends the office of their care and pain to have collected and published them.

Nor can an editor, after he has done his best, forget Heminges and Condell's final words: "And so we leave you to other of his friends, whom if you need can be your guides. If you need them not, you can lead yourselves, and others. And such readers we wish him."

SYLVAN BARNET
Tufts University

Introduction

It has been customary since the late nineteenth century to call *All's Well That Ends Well* a "problem play," or a "dark comedy." The first term relates it to the sort of drama we associate chiefly with Ibsen, a play about a social system in need of repair, a system with, say, faulty attitudes toward female emancipation or toward venereal disease. Because *All's Well* (like much other Elizabethan comedy) includes speeches on the nature of virtue and presents us with a picture of a virtuous but lowborn woman rejected by her snobbish husband, there was enough point in the comparison to give it some life for more than half a century. But what is the problem? Because Shakespeare's Helena seemed to resemble Ibsen's Nora, *All's Well* gained Shaw's approval (as much of Shakespeare did not), but it is not really very like a nineteenth-century *pièce à thèse*. It does not move toward a debate in which some commonly held code is called into doubt; it does not preach the abandonment of humbug; it does not suggest that the world will go well if only people will give up romantic ideas. It does not really anatomize the problem of nobility —Does nobility reside in lineage or in deeds?—because the lowborn heroine is so clearly right and the snobbish aristocrat so clearly wrong that there is no debate.

Abandoning the hunt for this sort of "problem," then, we can turn to a different sort of problem that has vexed students of the play: Where does it fit in Shakespeare's career? Here we confront the term "dark comedy," which associates this play with an alleged period in Shakespeare's life, about 1601–06, when he supposedly lost faith in the golden world he had seen about him (and had dramatized in *A Midsummer Night's Dream, As You Like It,* and *Twelfth Night*) and fell into the bitter cynicism that— users of the term commonly say—marks this play as well as *Measure for Measure, Troilus and Cressida, Hamlet, King Lear,* and *Timon of Athens.* The late E. K. Chambers—a great scholar, with whom one may differ only humbly and reluctantly—in *Shakespeare: A Survey* puts it this way: *All's Well*

> groups itself undeniably with *Troilus and Cressida* and *Measure for Measure,* as one of the bitter comedies; for it is a comedy from which all laughter has evaporated, save the grim laughter which follows the dubious sallies of Monsieur Lavache and the contemptuous laughter which presides over the plucking bare of the ineffable Parolles. The spiritual affinities of Helena's story are indeed far less with the radiant humor of *Twelfth Night* and *As You Like It* than with the analytic psychology of the great advance-guard of tragedy, *Julius Caesar* and *Hamlet,* which was almost contemporary with these.

The theory runs that for some reason Shakespeare became unhappy and turned to tragedy and to bitter comedy. Why he did so is variously explained. For some proponents, the sonnets tell a story of the poet's discovery of betrayal; the friend's infidelity, or the Dark Lady's lust, drove Shakespeare to despair, and the despair is manifested in the plays. Or the fall of Essex shattered Shakespeare's world. (Chambers very tentatively inclines to the suggestion that "Shakespeare's world-sickness" may be most plausibly related to the failure of Essex's conspiracy.) Or the death of Shakespeare's father in 1601 was a crushing blow. Or the advent of the unimpressive James I, following the death of Queen Elizabeth in 1603, was enough to cause the poet great unhappiness. But all these speculations are based on the shaky premise that a professional dramatist's works mirror his state of mind, as a romantic lyric poet's are supposed to. He writes tragedies when tragedy has struck home, and he writes comedies when all is going well. Probably an Elizabethan dramatist would have been surprised to learn that he had been writing autobiography when all along he had thought he was writing tragedy, comedy, history, or whatever else his company wanted or was currently in vogue.

The play was first published in the Folio of 1623, seven years after Shakespeare's death. There is no external evidence of the date of *All's Well*—no reference to it by any witness, no quotation from it in a datable work, no detected allusion in it to any current event. Conjectures about its date must be based on theories about Shakespeare's progressive use of certain motifs and the development of Shakespeare's style.

To take the question of motif first: most readers find the bed trick, or the "substitute bride motif" (to use the delicate term that folklorists apply to stories in which a wife substitutes herself for another woman to deceive her would-be adulterous husband), so arresting that the play is felt to closely resemble *Measure for Measure,* in which Angelo beds with Mariana, to whom he was betrothed, rather than with Isabella, whom he thinks he has seduced. In *All's Well,* the caddish Bertram vows he will not live with his wife Helena until she can get a ring from his finger and show him a child she has had by him; Helena, taking advantage of Bertram's illicit interest in the chaste Diana, is at length able to fulfill these seemingly impossible conditions. Shakespeare, however, was a great user and re-user of folk motifs, and there is really not much strength in the argument that because the "substitute bride" is used in *All's Well* the play must be close in date to *Measure for Measure,* given at court in December, 1604. After all, there is a tale of shipwreck at the start of *The Comedy of Errors* and there is an apparent shipwreck at the start of *The Tempest,* but some twenty years separate the two. Similarly, there are outlaws in *The Two Gentlemen of Verona* and in *As You Like It,* but no one would seriously argue that the plays were written in close proximity. On the other hand, *The Comedy of Errors* and *Love's Labor's Lost*—universally agreed to be among Shakespeare's earliest work—share no common motifs; *Love's Labor's Lost* does not even conclude with the unions or reunions that are almost the *sine qua non* of Shakespeare's comedies.

The bed trick in *Measure for Measure* is managed not by the bride but by a duke who advises her how to outwit a would-be seducer. The bed trick in *All's Well* is the bride's idea, and in its clever heroine *All's Well* differs from *Measure for Measure* and resembles the earlier comedies: *The Merchant of Venice* (in which Portia is more resourceful than all the Venetian men), *As You Like It* (in which Rosalind, banished to the woods, manipulates two weddings), and *Twelfth Night* (in which Viola at length weds the man whom she has loved for four and a half acts). Like these comedies, moreover, *All's Well* is a play about love and marriage: the "dark" *Troilus and Cressida,* less about love than about dishonor and disillusion, concludes with the lovers separated; *Measure for Measure* concludes with a strong hint of a marriage but the play is less about love than it is about lust and justice and mercy.

The subject matter offers no compelling argument to date the play later than the "happy" comedies and along with *Measure for Measure,* but there are abundant passages in a style more mature than the style (or, rather, styles) typical of the earliest plays. Much of the verse in *All's Well* has a complexity, weightiness, and forcefulness that resemble the verse in *Hamlet* and *Measure for Measure.* Here are two examples:

> Why not a mother? When I said "a mother"
> Methought you saw a serpent. What's in "mother"
> That you start at it? I say I am your mother,
> And put you in the catalogue of those
> That were enwombèd mine. Tis often seen
> Adoption strives with nature, and choice breeds
> A native slip to us from foreign seeds.
> You ne'er oppressed me with a mother's groan,
> Yet I express to you a mother's care.   (I.iii.142–50)

> That thou didst love her, strikes some scores away
> From the great compt; but love that comes too late,

Like a remorseful pardon slowly carried,
To the great sender turns a sour offense,
Crying "That's good that's gone." Our rash faults
Make trivial price of serious things we have,
Not knowing them, until we know their grave.

(V.iii.56–62)

But this business of choosing passages is tricky; no play
is all of a piece, and in selecting these a fair number in a
different style were skipped. There are more than a few
passages that are so simple, so jingling, so unsophisticated
that they seem like apprentice work:

If she, my liege, can make me know this clearly,
I'll love her dearly, ever, ever dearly.   (V.iii.315–16)

Here is my hand; the premises observed,
Thy will by my performance shall be served;
So make the choice of thy own time, for I,
Thy resolved patient, on thee still rely.
More should I question thee, and more I must,
Though more to know could not be more to trust.

(II.i.203–08)

Various explanations can be offered for the rhymes—that
here they add to a sense of ritual, that there they are used
for a letter (which must be set off), that they deal with
the past, that they make a contrast with a previous speech,
that they are vestiges of an old play Shakespeare is re-
vising, etc.—but the fact remains that the style is not sufficiently uniform to allow the easy generalization that it
resembles the style of *Measure for Measure*. The most
noticeable sign of maturity is the high percentage of run-
on lines (giving a flexibility and power lacking in much
of the early highly regular verse)—but this percentage is
not significantly different from that in *The Merchant of
Venice,* published in 1598 and quite possibly written a
year or two earlier. It should be mentioned, too, that some
of the least slick, the most "weighty" passages in *All's
Well* may owe part of their weight to the fact that the

printer did not correctly decipher the manuscript; the text is not a particularly good one, and some of the obscurity (often associated with maturity) perhaps has its origin in printing house uncertainties.

"Obscurity" gets us back to the idea of a "dark" play. The bed trick has seemed unpleasant to most readers (though it should be noted that by this trick Helena saves Bertram from committing adultery, and ultimately restores to him the wife who, we have seen, is a loving as well as an enterprising woman), but no one in the play minds it. The virtuous widow, who would avoid "any staining act," pronounces the plan "lawful," and the King is sufficiently delighted by the outcome to reward the widow's daughter. The other allegedly "dark" aspect of the play that has attracted a good deal of comment is the beginning, which is weighty with talk of death and disease:

> *Countess.* In delivering my son from me I bury a second husband.
> *Bertram.* And I in going, madam, weep o'er my father's death anew; but I must attend his Majesty's command. . . .
> *Countess.* What hope is there of his Majesty's amendment?
> *Lafew.* He hath abandoned his physicians. . . .

The play goes on, with talk of "haggish age" that has brought about the King's illness, the death of Bertram's father, and presumably the death of Helena's father. Yet how do Elizabethan comedies usually open if not with some sorrowful problem at hand, whose dissolution will be the matter of the play? The first speech in *The Comedy of Errors* is a couplet spoken by a man who knows he will be sentenced to death (it contains the words "fall," "doom of death," and "woes"); when he is assured that he is indeed sentenced to death, he tells a woeful tale of shipwreck and separation from wife and children. *The Two Gentlemen of Verona* begins with friends separating; *Love's Labor's Lost* begins with a vigorous speech announcing a method of securing eternal fame, but this very speech is full of awareness of "brazen tombs," "disgrace of death," and "cormorant devouring Time." The fact is that the first scene of *All's Well* mingles with its references to sorrow references to renewal, rebirth—the happy ending that characterizes comedy. The Countess is losing her son, but she is assured she will find in the King "a husband"; Helena's father has died, but his prescription lives in papers that Helena possesses, and the King will soon be restored to health. Helena seems to be grieving for her dead father, but in fact her mind is on the young man whom she loves, and though her love seems hopeless she wins him as her husband. If *As You Like It* included the bed trick, which is to say if Orlando were a cad, quite possibly the embarrassed and unhappy critics would have found that play, commonly called happy and golden, as dark as *All's Well*. After all, *As You Like It* begins with the bitter complaints of a younger brother, quickly moves to a fight between the brothers and to some churlish words ("old dog") spoken to an aged faithful retainer, and then to news that the rightful duke has been banished by his brother: family treachery, the tragic stuff that makes *King Lear*. Of course Bertram, the young lover in *All's Well,* is far less engaging than Orlando, but several of Shakespeare's lovers are unamiable people (Proteus in *The Two Gentlemen,* Claudio in *Much Ado*), yet the comedies are not therefore dark. (It can even be argued that Lysander's delightful transient infidelity in *A Midsummer Night's Dream* has its affinity with Bertram's perverse desire to seduce Diana when he is furnished with Helena, but it must be admitted that the spirit of holiday foolery, dominant in *A Midsummer Night's Dream,* is sparse in *All's Well.*)

An old theory, now rarely held because of the tendency to call it a problem play and to date it about 1602, suggests that *All's Well That Ends Well* is the play Francis Meres called *Love Labor's Won* when he listed a dozen of Shakespeare's plays in 1598. Meres says that Shakespeare excels both in comedy and tragedy:

For comedy, witness his *Gentlemen of Verona,* his *Er-*

rors, his *Love Labor's Lost,* his *Love Labor's Won,* his
Midsummer's Night Dream, and his *Merchant of Venice;*
for tragedy his *Richard the Second, Richard the Third,
Henry the Fourth, King John, Titus Andronicus,* and his
Romeo and Juliet.

Of these, only *Love Labor's Won* has not come down to
us, or has not come down to us under that title. If Meres
was not mistaken (he seems to know what he is talking
about), and Shakespeare had indeed written the play, it
is reasonable to assume that it is included in the Folio,
but under a different title. (The Folio was prepared by
long-standing friends of Shakespeare, who sought to col-
lect his plays as his memorial.) *The Taming of the Shrew*
has been the favorite candidate because it is unquestion-
ably early enough for Meres to have known of it in 1598,
but the recent discovery of a page from an account book
for 1603 lists—among other plays—both *The Taming of
the Shrew* and *Love's Labor Won* (sic), and so the two
cannot be identical. The plot of *All's Well* makes it an
eminently suitable candidate; Helena certainly labors to
win her beloved. If the identity of *All's Well* and *Love's
Labor's Won* (to combine Meres's spelling and that of the
account book) were established, it would prove that
All's Well had been written by 1598 and published by
1603—but no proof is available. Put it this way: if
Meres was correct that Shakespeare wrote *Love's Labor's
Won,* quite possibly it survives (presumably with substantial revision) as *All's Well,* and we should alter our con-
ception of Shakespeare's development; but if Meres was
mistaken, and the play was by another hand (hence omit-
ted from the Folio), we have been wasting our time.

Although the play dramatizes the triumph of love's
labor, Helena engages in activities that have distressed
some readers. Her dialogue with Parolles (I.i.) in which
she bandies jokes about virginity may seem neither witty
nor decorous to us, but we ought to recall that Bassanio's
Portia, a paragon, makes off-color jokes, as do several of
Shakespeare's other chaste comic heroines. This dialogue,
moreover, is not mere irrelevant foolery; Helena insists

that she will maintain her chastity awhile, as a virtuous heroine should, and the dialogue concludes with Parolles' advice, "Get thee a good husband, and use him as he uses thee." The play deals with Helena's getting a husband; in one sense she does not use him as he uses her (she returns his scorn with love); in another sense she does, for she deceives him—to a good end—as he deceives her. He accepts her as his wife but fabricates a means of leaving her without consummating the marriage, and she fabricates a means of saving him from adultery and of guiding him into what we must assume will be (as in the world of all comedy) a marriage in which they live happily ever after. That Helena engages in deception is not in itself bad. Deception in Elizabethan drama is commonly used to assist a love affair. No one is upset by the "honest slanders" devised to bring Beatrice and Benedick together in *Much Ado,* and the list of heroines who in one way or another deceive their beloved for a good purpose is a long one. Helena takes advantage of Bertram's pursuit of Diana to substitute herself for Diana:

> Why then tonight
> Let us assay our plot, which, if it speed,
> Is wicked meaning in a lawful deed,
> And lawful meaning in a lawful act,
> Where both not sin, and yet a sinful fact.
>
>   (III.vii.43–47)

Because Bertram intends adultery, for him it will be a "wicked meaning," but it will be a lawful deed because a chaste wife will be in bed with her husband; it will be, for Helena, a "lawful meaning in a lawful act," and though Bertram will think he is sinning, there is no sin because he and his partner are husband and wife. Bertram is an "unseasoned courtier," a foolish young prig whom Helena must bring to a healthy condition (he has "sick desires" for Diana) rather as she must heal the King's disease. Like Shakespeare's better-known heroines, Rosalind, Portia, Beatrice, and Viola, Helena is energetic yet thoroughly womanly. If one thinks she is too inclined to

wear the pants, what of Julia, Rosalind, and Viola, all
of whom—unlike Helena—literally wear pants in their
efforts to bring matters to a happy ending? Helena has
something of the earnestness of Brutus' Portia combined
with the resourcefulness of Bassanio's Portia; she fears
that her "ambitious love" has "offended," and that
Bertram is "too good and fair" for her, but no character
except Bertram ever speaks ill of her, and it is evident to
all readers that Bertram is (until at the end when he
accepts Helena) far from "good and fair."

Perhaps our chief dissatisfaction with Helena arises
from the fact that we cannot laugh at her—unless we feel
that Parolles has the better of the argument on virginity.
Rosalind (to give only one example) is engaging partly
because we enjoy her discomfort when she learns that her
beloved Orlando is in the Forest of Arden:

> Alas the day! What shall I do with my doublet and hose?
> What did he when thou saw'st him? What said he? How
> looked he? Wherein went he? What makes he here? Did
> he ask for me? Where remains he? How parted he with
> thee? And when shalt thou see him again? Answer me
> in one word.   (III.ii.217–22)

We get nothing like this, and we miss it. But if we never
experience the delightful intimacy of laughing at one with
whom we sympathize, it does not follow that we must
find Helena an unpleasant man-hunter. She feigns death—
but in *Much Ado* and in *A Winter's Tale* similar false
reports of death are issued for the good purpose of re-
storing a man to his loving wife. The women in those
two plays do not themselves contrive the report, but no
discredit accrues to the contrivers and none ought to
accrue to Helena. It is better to say that Helena resource-
fully persists in love than that (E. K. Chambers' words)
she "passes from dishonor to dishonor."

The offensive person in the play is not Helena, who
loves Bertram and brings him to love her, but Bertram,
whose folly is abundantly remarked upon. His mother,
Lafew, and the King all rebuke him, and though one can

sympathize with his plea that in the choice of a wife he might reasonably be allowed the help of his own eyes, it is clear that he is blind—not only to Helena's goodness but to Parolles' folly. Bertram believes that the cowardly braggart Parolles is a soldier simply because he talks and dresses the part. Bertram squares his guesses by shows (to take a line that appears in another context), values the worthless Parolles and (a sort of corollary) scorns the virtuous Helena. Fortunately, he lives in the world of comedy; "comedy is full of purposes mistook, not 'falling on the inventor's head' but luckily misfiring altogether. In comedy, as often happens in life, people are mercifully saved from being as wicked as they meant to be."[1]

It is commonly said that the world of *All's Well,* like that of *Measure for Measure,* is a depraved place, a cynic's vision—again the "dark" realm of an embittered writer. Readers of the Signet edition of the latter play may also have read an appended essay by R. W. Chambers (not to be confused with E. K. Chambers); if so, they will not be likely to see *Measure for Measure* as "dark." Nor is the world of *All's Well* wretched. Bertram is a fool, Parolles is close to a scoundrel, but the rest of the characters—including the Clown, whose bawdry is playful enough—are tolerable and tolerant, endowed with no more than the usual faults of men, and (if we keep in mind Helena, Lafew, the King, and the Countess) with more than the usual virtues. Bertram's failure to value Helena and his failure to see through Parolles are abundantly remarked upon, but when Parolles has been exposed and Helena is reputed dead, and nothing can come of further dwelling on Bertram's past folly, Lafew, the Countess, and the King forgive him. Lafew asserts that Bertram was "misled with [i.e., by] a snipped taffeta fellow," the Countess (who had spoken sharply to Bertram when sharp-speaking might have been of some use) now urges the King "to make it/Natural rebellion done i' th' blade of youth,/When oil and fire, too strong

[1] Helen Gardner, "As You Like It," in *More Talking of Shakespeare,* ed. John Garret. This essay is reprinted in the Signet edition of *As You Like It.*

for reason's force,/O'erbears it and burns on," and the King replies that he has "forgiven and forgotten all." Indeed, despite his immaturity Bertram has won repute in battle and now, apparently aware of his opprobrious behavior, he begs pardon for his "high-repented blames." It is recognized that Bertram has done abundant wrong to the King, to his mother, to Helena, and

> to himself
> The greatest wrong of all. He lost a wife
> Whose beauty did astonish the survey
> Of richest eyes; whose words all ears took captive;
> Whose dear perfection hearts that scorned to serve
> Humbly called mistress.   (V.iii.14–19)

But this greatest wrong has not in fact been done; love and Providence have contrived that all shall end well. "What things are we!" exclaims the First Lord, and the Second Lord replies:

> Merely our own traitors. And as in the common course of all treasons we still see them reveal themselves till they attain to their abhorred ends, so he that in this action contrives against his own nobility, in his proper stream o'erflows himself.   (IV.iii.22–27)

In another context this is the stuff of tragedy. Macbeth, for example, urged by his wife, contrives against his own nobility and destroys himself. The violence he does to his king recoils upon him and he finds he has achieved not "honor, love, obedience, troops of friends," but only curses, false friends, and sleepless nights. In *All's Well* men are not angels, but neither are they devils; love and forgiveness are no less evident than folly and youthful lust. The vision is no darker than that radiant moment in *The Merchant of Venice* when Portia, appealing to Shylock to show mercy toward the man who has indeed forfeited his bond, says:

> Though justice be thy plea, consider this:

That, in the course of justice, none of us
Should see salvation. We do pray for mercy,
And that same prayer doth teach us all to render
The deeds of mercy.   (IV.i.197–201)

The world of *The Merchant of Venice* is more lyrical,
filled with moonlight and music—when Shylock is not
onstage—but the vision of humanity is no higher; lower,
indeed, for Shylock is malevolent where Bertram and
Parolles are foolish. In Shakespeare's comedies, folly is
not something scourged but something enjoyed. For example, in *Love's Labor's Lost,* a delightful spoof on the
folly of trying to live as though men were disembodied
minds, the King of Navarre, leader of the scheme to
form a society of scholars who shall give no audience to
women, proudly tells his followers that they "war against
affections [i.e., passions],/And the huge army of the
world's desire." How noble, and yet how foolish. Nor is
it cynical to say that this is folly; Berowne aptly points
out that "every man with his affects is born,/Not by
might mastered, but by special grace," and as though to
prove his point a constable brings in a clown who has
already broken the vow to forswear women. The affects
have their place, no less than reason. Even our faults can
serve us. "The web of our life," says a French lord in
All's Well, "is of a mingled yarn, good and ill together;
our virtues would be proud if our faults whipped them
not, and our crimes would despair if they were not cherished by our virtues" (IV.iii.74–78). If mortals are
fools, Shakespeare seems to cherish them as much for
their folly as Puck does, and (notably in *Much Ado,*
where the clowns bring about the denouement) he turns
their folly to use. The delightful thing about folly is that
it insulates a man from despair and fills him with a zest
for living. Othello's occupation is gone when Desdemona
is (he thinks) unfaithful, but Parolles can easily enough
find another livelihood when his military claims are
exposed.

If my heart were great

'Twould burst at this. Captain I'll be no more,
But I will eat and drink and sleep as soft
As captain shall. Simply the thing I am
Shall make me live. Who knows himself a braggart,
Let him fear this; for it will come to pass
That every braggart shall be found an ass.
Rust, sword; cool, blushes; and Parolles live
Safest in shame! Being fooled, by fool'ry thrive!
There's place and means for every man alive.
I'll after them.   *Exit.*
                                    (IV.iii.345–55)

Othello kills himself, "for he was great of heart," but Parolles is protected from Othello's greatness ("*If* my heart were great") and therefore from murdering a Desdemona and from committing suicide. Lafew, who had been the first to detect Parolles, treats him generously enough at last: "Though you are a fool and a knave you shall eat." Parolles, indeed, in the final act becomes an engaging fool; another comic dramatist would have whipped him from the stage, but Shakespeare exposes Parolles not merely for moral reasons but "for the love of laughter" (twice repeated), and finds a place for the braggart-turned-fool in the abundant comic world.

All ends well, partly because most of the people in the play are decent, but chiefly because of a beneficent Providence. By the time the play reaches its end, not only has the King been restored to health, Parolles cured of his pretensions, Diana equipped with a dowry, Bertram brought to his senses, but Helena is wed in deed as well as name to a loving husband. Now, it is the nature of a play, or any work of art, in contrast to real life, that the doings of the characters are remarkably coherent. In the theater we look attentively for a few hours at a few people and we see the course of a lifetime, or all that presumably is significant in a lifetime, whereas in life things go on for years, mingled with a good deal of irrelevance. Life may or may not be a chaos; art is a pattern. Something like Fate presides in all plays, however vivid and energetic the characters may be. "Hanging and wiving goes by destiny," Nerissa lightly says, providing us with a tag that summarizes tragedy and comedy. "Who can control his fate?" Othello asks. Surely not the tragic heroes—unless we see them as men who get exactly what they deserve. No less than five of Euripides' plays include (with one variation) these lines:

> Many indeed the shapes and changes are
> Of heavenly beings. Many things the gods
> Achieve beyond our judgment. What we thought
> Is not confirmed, and what we thought not God
> Contrives. And so it happens in this story.[2]

The comic version of Fate is Fortune or Time or beneficent Providence:

> All other doubts, by Time let them be cleared.
> Fortune brings in some boats that are not steered.
> (*Cymbeline*, IV.iii)

> O Time, thou must untangle this, not I;
> It is too hard a knot for me t' untie.
> (*Twelfth Night*, II.ii)

In *All's Well*, numerous references to Providence make explicit the pattern that underlies all comedy. "The very hand of heaven" cures the King. Later, Helena is providentially brought to the very place and persons that can restore her to Bertram:

> Doubt not but heaven
> Hath brought me up to be your daughter's dower,
> As it hath fated her to be my motive [i.e., means]
> And helper to a husband. (IV.iv.18–21)

In Shakespeare's source, the heroine "purposed to find means to attain the two things, that thereby she might recover her husband," and she set out for Florence. But in *All's Well*, when Helena sets out on her pilgrimage to

[2] Translation by Rex Warner, in *Three Great Plays of Euripides*, New York: The New American Library of World Literature, Inc. (Mentor Books), 1958.

St. Jaques we are not given any reason to believe that she is pursuing Bertram. Learning of the seemingly impossible conditions Bertram has imposed, she says almost nothing, allowing the Countess and others to censure him. When the Countess and Lords leave the stage, in a soliloquy she blames herself for driving Bertram to the wars where he may "be the mark/Of smoky muskets."

> Shall I stay here to do't? No, no, although
> The air of paradise did fan the house
> And angels officed all. I will be gone,
> That pitiful rumor may report my flight
> To consolate thine ear. Come night, end day;
> For with the dark, poor thief, I'll steal away.
> *Exit.*
> (III.ii.129–34)

We learn (from a letter) that she has set out on a pilgrimage, and that Bertram may thus return to Rousillon. We next meet Helena in Florence, where by chance she engages in conversation a widow who, as it turns out, is the mother of a young girl whom Bertram is courting. We have no right to assume that Helena lied in her soliloquy (to whom could she be lying?) and that she set out to catch Bertram; we can only assume that the hand of heaven has brought about the encounter in Florence with the widow, her daughter, and Bertram. It is worth mentioning, too, that in the source the heroine meets a Florentine woman who leads her to the widow, but Shakespeare's Helena happens on the widow unaided. The effect is to increase the sense of Providence precisely because it is so improbable that Helena would encounter the widow herself. To say that in *All's Well* there is often a sense of Providence is not, of course, to say that the characters are mindless puppets who undertake nothing for themselves. Helena herself argues (I.i.223–36) to the contrary. Readiness, however, is all:

> But with the word the time will bring on summer,
> When briars shall have leaves as well as thorns,

And be as sweet as sharp. We must away;
Our wagon is prepared, and time revives us.
All's well that ends well; still the fine's the crown.
Whate'er the course, the end is the renown.

(IV.iv.31–36)

("The fine's the crown" is an idea Shakespeare stated
more than once; in the second part of *Henry VI* we get
"La fin couronne les oeuvres," in *Troilus* "The end
crowns all"; elsewhere there are variations.) The co-
operation with time that Helena here urges she urges
again at Marseilles, when the widow despairs that they
have come too late.

Widow. Lord, how we lose our pains!

Helena. All's well that ends well yet,
    Though time seems so adverse and means unfit.
    I do beseech you, whither is he gone?
* * * * * * * * * *
                  We must to horse again.

(V.i.24–37)

In V.iii the King forgives Bertram and observes that
"The time is fair again":

                  All is whole.
    Not one word more of the consumèd time.
    Let's take the instant by the forward top;
    For we are old, and on our quick'st decrees
    Th' inaudible and noiseless foot of Time
    Steals ere we can effect them.   (V.iii.37–42)

But the time (here, with a suggestion of the age, the
present state) is not yet "whole," for Helena is still
thought dead, hence the appropriateness of the melancholy
note introduced by the King's reflections on his old age.
The melancholy deepens as thoughts return to the "dead"
Helena, whom Bertram now laments. The King repeats
his forgiveness:

                  Well excused.

> That thou didst love her, strikes some scores away
> From the great compt; but love that comes too late,
> Like a remorseful pardon slowly carried,
> To the great sender turns a sour offense,
> Crying "That's good that's gone."   (V.iii.55–60)

Reluctantly skipping this near-chance to compare the motif of "That's good that's gone" with its occurrence in the tragedies, notably in *Antony and Cleopatra,* we move on and note that the last lines in the play (excluding the epilogue) are:

> All yet seems well, and if it end so meet,
> The bitter past, more welcome is the sweet.

The tragic lesson that the Greek dramatists often preached was "Count no man happy until he is dead"; Oedipus *seemed* happy, but because he had killed his father and married his mother he was a contaminated wretch whose *life* was tragic though he did not know it until near the end of the play. His actions (to borrow from Aristotle's ethical theories) were not in accordance with virtue and therefore he was not genuinely happy. Conversely, in *All's Well,* though Helena is dogged by misfortune, and Bertram is for a while a fool, Helena's persistent virtue, in combination with God's grace, saves Bertram from himself and brings happiness to herself and to a variety of lesser characters. "Choose thou thy husband," the delighted King says to Diana, "and I'll pay thy dower." All has ended well, which means that a happy *beginning* is in store for Helena and Bertram, and for Diana and whomever she elects. Correspondingly, the end of the play glances back to the beginning. The King's invitation to Diana to choose a husband echoes his earlier agreement to let Helena choose a husband. Still another link between end and beginning is found in the epilogue; the King says,

> The King's a beggar now the play is done,

appealing to the audience for applause, but in his sudden loss of power our minds may travel back to the weak king in the first act; and in the full realization that he is a king only in so far as our imagination takes his clothing to be an external symbol of an internal reality, we may recall that Parolles' military garb covered nothing substantial. The story is over, the characters live happily ever after, disembodied from the actors who have presented them and who in the workaday world daily—"with strife"—seek to please the audience. For a moment the audience becomes a benevolent Providence, governing the figures on the stage by bestowing the applause which allows them to depart.

SYLVAN BARNET

All's Well
That Ends Well

[*Dramatis Personae*

King of France
Duke of Florence
Bertram, Count of Rousillon
Lafew, an old lord
Parolles, a follower of Bertram
Steward, named Rinaldo ⎱
Clown, named Lavatch ⎰ servants to the Countess
A Page ⎰
Two French lords, the brothers Dumaine, serving in the
    Florentine army
A Gentleman, a stranger
Countess of Rousillon, mother to Bertram
Helena, an orphan protected by the Countess
A Widow of Florence
Diana, daughter to the widow
Mariana, neighbor to the widow
Lords, Officers, Soldiers, Attendants

Scene: Rousillon; Paris; Florence; Marseilles]

All's Well That Ends Well

ACT I

Scene I. [*Rousillon.*°¹ *The Count's palace.*]

*Enter young Bertram, Count of Rousillon, his
mother [the Countess], and Helena, Lord Lafew,
all in black.*

Countess. In delivering° my son from me I bury a
second husband.

Bertram. And I in going, madam, weep o'er my
father's death anew; but I must attend his Majesty's
command, to whom I am now in ward,° evermore   5
in subjection.

Lafew. You shall find of° the King a husband,
madam; you, sir, a father. He that so generally°
is at all times good must of necessity hold° his
virtue to you, whose worthiness would stir it up   10

---

¹ The degree sign (°) indicates a footnote, which is keyed to the
text by line number. Text references are printed in boldface; the
annotation follows in roman type. **I.i.s.d. Rousillon** formerly a
province in southern France (usually spelled "Rossillion" in the
Folio; the accent is on the second syllable, and -llion was probably
pronounced -yun)   1 **delivering** sending away (with pun on giving
birth)   5 **to whom I am now in ward** whose ward I now am   7 **of**
in   8 **generally** impartially   9 **hold** continue

where it wanted,° rather than lack it where there
is such abundance.

Countess. What hope is there of his Majesty's amend-
ment?

15 *Lafew.* He hath abandoned his physicians, madam,
under whose practices he hath persecuted time with
hope, and finds no other advantage in the process
but only the losing of hope by time.

Countess. This young gentlewoman had a father—O,
20   that "had," how sad a passage° 'tis—whose skill
was almost as great as his honesty; had it stretched
so far, would have made nature immortal, and
death should have play for lack of work. Would
for the King's sake he were living! I think it would
25   be the death of the King's disease.

Lafew. How called you the man you speak of,
madam?

Countess. He was famous, sir, in his profession, and
it was his great right to be so: Gerard de Narbon.

30 *Lafew.* He was excellent indeed, madam. The King
very lately spoke of him admiringly and mourn-
ingly; he was skillful enough to have lived still, if
knowledge could be set up against mortality.

Bertram. What is it, my good lord, the King lan-
35   guishes of?

Lafew. A fistula,° my lord.

Bertram. I heard not of it before.

Lafew. I would it were not notorious. Was this gentlewoman the daughter of Gerard de Narbon?

40 *Countess.* His sole child, my lord, and bequeathed to
my overlooking.° I have those hopes of her good

---

11 **where it wanted** i.e., even if it (virtue) were lacking   20 **passage**
(1) incident (2) passing away   36 **fistula** abscess   41 **overlooking**
guardianship

that her education promises; her dispositions she
inherits, which makes fair gifts fairer; for where an
unclean mind carries virtuous qualities,° there commendations go with pity; they are virtues and
traitors too. In her they are the better for their
simpleness;° she derives° her honesty and achieves
her goodness.

Lafew. Your commendations, madam, get from her
tears.

Countess. 'Tis the best brine a maiden can season°
her praise in. The remembrance of her father never
approaches her heart but the tyranny of her sorrows takes all livelihood° from her cheek. No more
of this, Helena; go to,° no more, lest it be rather
thought you affect° a sorrow than to have—

Helena. I do affect a sorrow indeed, but I have it
too.

Lafew. Moderate lamentation is the right of the dead,
excessive grief the enemy to the living.

Countess. If the living be enemy to the grief, the ex-
cess makes it soon mortal.

Bertram. Madam, I desire your holy wishes.

Lafew. How understand we that?°

Countess. Be thou blessed, Bertram, and succeed
　　thy father
In manners° as in shape! Thy° blood and virtue
Contend for empire in thee, and thy goodness

45

50

55

60

65

---

44 **virtuous qualities** skills (not moral qualities)　46–47 **their simpleness** being single, unmixed　47 **derives** inherits　51 **season** preserve
54 **livelihood** (1) vitality (2) nourishment　55 **go to** (a remonstrance,
"Stop")　56 **affect** feign (Helena enigmatically replies that she both
feigns a sorrow—for her father, we later learn—and has one; her use
of the word also includes another meaning, "love")　64 **Lafew . . .
that** (perhaps this line is misplaced, and should begin Lafew's previous speech)　66 **manners** morals　66 **Thy** may thy

    Share with thy birthright! Love all, trust a few,
    Do wrong to none; be able for thine enemy
70 Rather in power than use,° and keep thy friend
    Under thy own life's key. Be checked for silence,
    But never taxed° for speech. What heaven more will,
    That thee may furnish and my prayers pluck down,
    Fall on thy head! Farewell. My lord,
75 'Tis an unseasoned courtier; good my lord,
    Advise him.

Lafew.   He cannot want° the best
    That shall attend his love.

Countess. Heaven bless him! Farewell, Bertram.
                                 [*Exit.*]

Bertram. The best wishes that can be forged in your
80 thoughts be servants to you! [*To Helena*] Be comfortable° to my mother, your mistress, and make
    much of her.

Lafew. Farewell, pretty lady; you must hold the credit
    of your father.   [*Exit with Bertram.*]

85 *Helena.* O, were that all! I think not on my father,
    And these great tears grace his remembrance more
    Than those I shed for him. What was he like?
    I have forgot him; my imagination
    Carries no favor° in't but Bertram's.
90 I am undone; there is no living, none,
    If Bertram be away; 'twere all one
    That I should love a bright particular star,
    And think to wed it, he is so above me.
    In his bright radiance and collateral light
95 Must I be comforted, not in his sphere.°

69–70 **be able . . . use** let your strength equal your foe's in potentiality, but do not use it 72 **taxed** censured 76 **want** lack
81 **comfortable** comforting 89 **favor** (1) face (2) love token 94–95
In his bright . . . sphere i.e., I must content myself with his light, parallel to ("collateral") but above me; I cannot be in his orbit

Th' ambition in my love thus plagues itself:
The hind that would be mated by the lion
Must die for love. 'Twas pretty, though a plague,
To see him every hour, to sit and draw
His archèd brows, his hawking° eye, his curls,   *100*
In our heart's table;° heart too capable°
Of every line and trick of his sweet favor.
But now he's gone, and my idolatrous fancy°
Must sanctify his relics. Who comes here?

Enter Parolles.°

One that goes with him. I love him for his sake,   *105*
And yet I know him a notorious liar,
Think him a great way fool, solely a coward;
Yet these fixed evils sit so fit in him,
That they take place° when virtue's steely bones
Looks bleak i' th' cold wind; withal,° full oft we
  see   *110*
Cold wisdom waiting on superfluous folly.°

Parolles. Save° you, fair queen!

Helena. And you, monarch!

Parolles. No.

Helena. And no.   *115*

Parolles. Are you meditating on virginity?

Helena. Ay. You have some stain° of soldier in you;
let me ask you a question. Man is enemy to virginity; how may we barricado it against him?

Parolles. Keep him out.   *120*

Helena. But he assails; and our virginity, though valiant, in the defense yet is weak. Unfold to us some
warlike resistance.

---

100 **hawking** hawklike, keen   101 **table** flat surface on which a
picture is drawn   101–02 **capable/Of** receptive to   103 **fancy** lover's
fantasy   104 s.d. **Parolles** (cf. French *paroles*, "words," i.e., Talker,
Braggart)   109 **take place** find acceptance (?)   110 **withal** besides
111 **Cold ... folly** i.e., a threadbare wise servant attending on a rich
fool   112 **Save** God save   117 **stain** tincture

Parolles. There is none. Man, setting down before°
125   you, will undermine you and blow you up.°

Helena. Bless our poor virginity from underminers
and blowers-up! Is there no military policy how
virgins might blow up men?

Parolles. Virginity being blown down, man will quick-
130   lier be blown up;° marry,° in blowing him down
again, with the breach yourselves made you lose
your city. It is not politic in the commonwealth of
nature to preserve virginity. Loss of virginity is
rational increase, and there was never virgin got°
135   till virginity was first lost. That° you were made of
is metal° to make virgins. Virginity by being once
lost may be ten times found; by being ever kept
it is ever lost. 'Tis too cold a companion; away
with't!

140   *Helena.* I will stand for't a little, though therefore
I die a virgin.

Parolles. There's little can be said in't; 'tis against the
rule of nature. To speak on the part of virginity, is
to accuse your mothers, which is most infallible
145   disobedience. He that hangs himself is a virgin; virginity murders itself, and should be buried in high-
ways out of all sanctified limit,° as a desperate
offendress against nature. Virginity breeds mites,
much like a cheese, consumes itself to the very
150   paring, and so dies with feeding his own stomach.°
Besides, virginity is peevish, proud, idle, made of
self-love which is the most inhibited sin in the

---

124 **setting down before** laying siege to   125 **blow you up** (1) ex-
plode you (2) make you pregnant   130 **be blown up** be swollen, i.e.,
reach an orgasm   130 **marry** (a mild oath, "By the Virgin Mary")
134 **got** begotten   135 **That** that which   136 **metal** (1) substance
(2) coin (3) mettle, spirit   147 **sanctified limit** consecrated ground
150 **stomach** pride

canon.° Keep° it not; you cannot choose but lose
by't. Out with't! Within ten year it will make itself
ten, which is a goodly increase, and the principal   155
itself not much the worse. Away with't!

Helena. How might one do, sir, to lose it to her own
liking?

Parolles. Let me see. Marry, ill, to like him that ne'er
it likes. 'Tis a commodity will lose the gloss with   160
lying; the longer kept, the less worth. Off with't
while 'tis vendible; answer the time of request. Virginity, like an old courtier, wears her cap out of
fashion, richly suited, but unsuitable,° just like the
brooch and the toothpick, which wear not now.°   165
Your date is better in your pie and your porridge
than in your cheek; and your virginity, your old
virginity, is like one of our French withered pears:
it looks ill, it eats drily; marry, 'tis a withered pear;
it was formerly better; marry, yet 'tis a withered   170
pear. Will you anything with it?

Helena. Not my virginity yet!°
There shall your master have a thousand loves,
A mother, and a mistress, and a friend,
A phoenix,° captain, and an enemy,   175
A guide, a goddess, and a sovereign,
A counselor, a traitress, and a dear;
His humble ambition, proud humility;
His jarring, concord, and his discord, dulcet;
His faith, his sweet disaster;° with a world   180
Of pretty, fond, adoptious christendoms
That blinking Cupid gossips.° Now shall he—

152–53 **inhibited sin in the canon** prohibited sin in the Scripture
153 **Keep** hoard   164 **unsuitable** unfashionable   165 **wear not now**
are not now in fashion   172 **yet** (possibly there are missing some
ensuing lines in which Helena comments on Bertram's departure,
possibly the abrupt transition reveals that Helena's thoughts have
not been on Parolles' talk)   175 **phoenix** i.e., rarity (literally, a
fabulous bird)   180 **disaster** unfavorable star   181–82 **fond . . .
gossips** foolish, adopted names that blind ("blinking") Cupid gives
as godfather ("gossips")

I know not what he shall. God send him well!
The court's a learning place, and he is one—

185 *Parolles.* What one, i' faith?

Helena. That I wish well. 'Tis pity—

Parolles. What's pity?

Helena. That wishing well had not a body in't,
Which might be felt, that we, the poorer born,
190   Whose baser stars° do shut us up in wishes,
Might with effects of them follow our friends,
And show what we alone must think, which never
Returns us thanks.

Enter Page.

Page. Monsieur Parolles, my lord calls for you.
                                                    [*Exit.*]

195 *Parolles.* Little Helen, farewell. If I can remember
thee, I will think of thee at court.

Helena. Monsieur Parolles, you were born under a
charitable star.

Parolles. Under Mars, ay.

200 *Helena.* I especially think, under Mars.

Parolles. Why under Mars?

Helena. The wars hath so kept you under,° that you
must needs be born under Mars.

Parolles. When he was predominant.

205 *Helena.* When he was retrograde,° I think rather.

Parolles. Why think you so?

Helena. You go so much backward when you fight.

Parolles. That's for advantage.

Helena. So is running away, when fear proposes the

---

190 **baser stars** lower destinies   202 **under** in low fortune   205 **retrograde** moving backward (astrological term)

safety; but the composition° that your valor and fear   *210*
makes in you is a virtue of a good wing, and I like
the wear° well.

Parolles. I am so full of businesses, I cannot answer
thee acutely. I will return perfect courtier, in the
which my instruction shall serve to naturalize°   *215*
thee, so thou wilt be capable of a courtier's counsel,
and understand what advice shall thrust upon thee;
else thou diest in thine unthankfulness, and thine
ignorance makes thee away. Farewell. When thou
hast leisure, say thy prayers; when thou hast none,   *220*
remember thy friends. Get thee a good husband,
and use him as he uses thee. So, farewell.   [*Exit.*]

Helena. Our remedies oft in ourselves do lie,
  Which we ascribe to heaven; the fated sky°
  Gives us free scope; only doth backward pull   *225*
  Our slow designs when we ourselves are dull.
  What power is it which mounts my love so high,
  That makes me see, and cannot feed mine eye?
  The mightiest space in fortune nature brings
  To join like likes, and kiss like native° things.   *230*
  Impossible be strange attempts to those
  That weigh their pains in sense, and do suppose
  What hath been cannot be.° Who ever strove
  To show her merit that did miss her love?
  The King's disease—my project may deceive me,   *235*
  But my intents are fixed, and will not leave me.
                                        Exit.

---

210 **composition** (1) union, mixture (2) truce, surrender   212 **wear**
fashion (if "wing" has referred not only to Parolles' flight but to a
flap on his clothing, "wear" puns—like the modern "fashion"—on
habit and clothing)   215 **naturalize** familiarize   224 **fated sky** sky
(heaven) that exerts influence   230 **native** closely related   231–33
Impossible . . . cannot be i.e., remarkable deeds are impossible to
persons who cautiously calculate the efforts and who believe that
unusual happenings cannot take place

[Scene II. *Paris. The King's palace.*]

*Flourish° cornets. Enter the King of France with
letters, and divers Attendants.*

King. The Florentines and Senoys° are by th' ears,°
Have fought with equal fortune, and continue
A braving war.°

First Lord.   So 'tis reported, sir.

King. Nay, 'tis most credible. We here receive it
5   A certainty, vouched from our cousin° Austria,
With caution, that the Florentine will move° us
For speedy aid; wherein our dearest friend
Prejudicates the business, and would seem
To have us make denial.

First Lord.   His love and wisdom,
10   Approved° so to your Majesty, may plead
For amplest credence.

King.   He hath armed our answer,
And Florence is denied before he comes;
Yet, for our gentlemen that mean to see
The Tuscan service,° freely have they leave
To stand on either part.°

15 *Second Lord.*   It well may serve
A nursery° to our gentry, who are sick
For breathing° and exploit.

I.ii.s.d. **Flourish** musical notes heralding an important person
1 **Senoys** Sienese   1 **by th' ears** quarreling   3 **braving war** war of
challenges   5 **cousin** fellow sovereign   6 **move** petition   10 **Approved** proven   14 **The Tuscan service** the campaign in Tuscany
(N. Italy)   15 **stand on either part** serve on either side   16 **nursery**
training school   16–17 **sick/For breathing** eager for exercise

Enter Bertram, Lafew, and Parolles.

King.   What's he comes here?

First Lord. It is the Count Rousillon, my good lord,
  Young Bertram.

King.   Youth, thou bear'st thy father's face.
  Frank° nature, rather curious° than in haste,   20
  Hath well composed thee. Thy father's moral parts
  May'st thou inherit too! Welcome to Paris.

Bertram. My thanks and duty are your Majesty's.

King. I would I had that corporal soundness now,
  As when thy father and myself in friendship   25
  First tried our soldiership. He did look far
  Into the service of the time,° and was
  Disciplen of the bravest. He lasted long,
  But on us both did haggish age steal on,
  And wore us out of act.° It much repairs me   30
  To talk of your good father; in his youth
  He had the wit which I can well observe
  Today in our young lords; but they may jest
  Till their own scorn return to them unnoted
  Ere they can hide their levity in° honor.   35
  So like a courtier, contempt nor bitterness
  Were in his pride or sharpness; if they were,
  His equal had awaked them, and his honor,
  Clock to itself, knew the true minute when
  Exception° bid him speak, and at this time   40
  His tongue obeyed his hand. Who° were below him
  He used as creatures of another place,°
  And bowed his eminent top to their low ranks,
  Making them proud of his humility,
  In their poor praise he humbled. Such a man   45
  Might be a copy to these younger times;

20 **Frank** bounteous   20 **curious** careful   26–27 **He did . . . time** he
had insight into war (?) he served long in wars (?)   30 **act** action
35 **hide . . . in** i.e., join . . . with (?)   40 **Exception** disapproval
41 **Who** those who   42 **another place** i.e., a higher rank

Which, followed well, would demonstrate them
now
But goers backward.

Bertram.   His good remembrance, sir,
Lies richer in your thoughts than on his tomb;
50   So in approof lives not his epitaph
As in your royal speech.°

King. Would I were with him! He would always say—
Methinks I hear him now; his plausive° words
He scattered not in ears, but grafted them,
55   To grow there, and to bear—"Let me not live,"
This his good melancholy oft began,
On the catastrophe and heel of pastime,°
When it was out°—"Let me not live," quoth he,
"After my flame lacks oil, to be the snuff°
60   Of younger spirits, whose apprehensive° senses
All but new things disdain; whose judgments are
Mere fathers of their garments; whose constancies
Expire before their fashions." This he wished.
I, after him, do after him° wish too,
65   Since I nor wax nor honey can bring home,
I quickly were dissolvèd from my hive
To give some laborers room.

Second Lord.   You're loved, sir;
They that least lend it you shall lack you first.

King. I fill a place, I know't. How long is't, Count,
70   Since the physician at your father's died?
He was much famed.

Bertram.   Some six months since, my lord.

King. If he were living, I would try him yet.

50–51 **So . . . speech** i.e., the validity of his epitaph is in no way
better confirmed than in your words   53 **plausive** laudable   57 **On
. . . pastime** at the end ("catastrophe," "heel") of pleasure   58 **out**
ended (perhaps punning on the idea "out at heel")   59 **snuff** burnt
wick that causes the lamp to smell and smolder, preventing the lower
("younger") wick from burning brightly   60 **apprehensive** perceptive, apt   64 **after him . . . after him** later than he . . . in accordance
with him

Lend me an arm. The rest have worn me out
With several applications.° Nature and sickness
Debate it at their leisure. Welcome, Count,   75
My son's no dearer.

Bertram.   Thank your Majesty.
              Exit [the King with the rest]. Flourish.

[Scene III. *Rousillon. The Count's palace.*]

Enter Countess, Steward, and Clown.

Countess. I will now hear. What say you of this
  gentlewoman?

Steward. Madam, the care I have had to even° your
  content I wish might be found in the calendar° of
  my past endeavors, for then we wound our mod-   5
  esty, and make foul the clearness of our deserv-
  ings, when of ourselves we publish them.

Countess. What does this knave here? Get you gone,
  sirrah.° The complaints I have heard of you I do
  not all believe; 'tis my slowness that I do not, for   10
  I know you lack not folly to commit them, and
  have ability enough to make such knaveries yours.

Clown. 'Tis not unknown to you, madam, I am a
  poor fellow.

Countess. Well, sir.   15

---

74 **several applications** various treatments   I.iii.3 **even** make even,
satisfy   4 **calendar** record   9 **sirrah** (term of address used to an inferior)

Clown. No, madam, 'tis not so well that I am poor, though many of the rich are damned; but, if I may have your ladyship's good will to go to the world,° Isbel the woman and I will do° as we may.

20 *Countess.* Wilt thou needs be a beggar?

Clown. I do beg your good will in this case.

Countess. In what case?

Clown. In Isbel's case° and mine own. Service is no heritage,° and I think I shall never have the bless-
25 ing of God till I have issue o' my body; for they say barnes° are blessings.

Countess. Tell me thy reason why thou wilt marry.

Clown. My poor body, madam, requires it. I am driven on by the flesh, and he must needs go that
30 the devil drives.

Countess. Is this all your worship's reason?

Clown. Faith, madam, I have other holy reasons,° such as they are.

Countess. May the world know them?

35 *Clown.* I have been, madam, a wicked creature, as you and all flesh and blood are, and indeed I do marry that I may repent.

Countess. Thy marriage, sooner than thy wickedness.

Clown. I am out o' friends, madam, and I hope to
40 have friends for my wife's sake.

Countess. Such friends are thine enemies, knave.

Clown. Y'are shallow, madam, in great friends, for the knaves come to do that for me which I am

18 **go to the world** get married   19 **do** (punning on the bawdy meaning "have intercourse")   23 **case** (another bawdy pun, "pudendum")   23–24 **Service is no heritage** i.e., servants acquire no wealth (proverbial)   26 **barnes** bairns, children   32 **holy reasons** (probably there is a bawdy pun not only on "holy" but on "reasons," pronounced much like "raisings")

aweary of. He that ears° my land spares my team,
and gives me leave to in° the crop; if I be his   45
cuckold,° he's my drudge. He that comforts my
wife is the cherisher of my flesh and blood; he that
cherishes my flesh and blood loves my flesh and
blood; he that loves my flesh and blood is my
friend: ergo, he that kisses my wife is my friend.   50
If men could be contented to be what they are,
there were no fear in marriage; for young Charbon
the puritan and old Poysam° the papist, how-
some'er their hearts are severed in religion, their
heads are both one; they may jowl° horns to-   55
gether like any deer i' th' herd.

Countess. Wilt thou ever be a foul-mouthed and
calumnious knave?

Clown. A prophet I, madam, and I speak the truth
the next° way: 60

> For I the ballad will repeat,
>   Which men full true shall find,
> Your marriage comes by destiny,
>   Your cuckoo sings by kind.°

Countess. Get you gone, sir. I'll talk with you more   65
anon.

Steward. May it please you, madam, that he bid
Helen come to you. Of her I am to speak.

Countess. Sirrah, tell my gentlewoman I would speak
with her—Helen I mean.   70

Clown. Was this fair face the cause, quoth she,
>   Why the Grecians sackèd Troy?
> Fond° done, done fond,
>   Was this King Priam's joy?

---

44 ears plows   45 in bring in   46 cuckold deceived husband (tradi-
tionally said to wear horns)   52–53 Charbon . . . Poysam Flesh-
eater . . . Fish-eater (from French *chair bonne* = good flesh; *poisson*
= fish)   55 jowl knock   60 next nearest   64 by kind according to
nature (the cuckoo allegedly sang to men that they were cuckolds)
73 Fond foolishly

75   With that she sighèd as she stood,
                  With that she sighèd as she stood,
                     And gave this sentence° then:
                  Among nine bad if one be good,
                  Among nine bad if one be good,
80   There's yet one good in ten.

Countess. What, one good in ten? You corrupt the
     song, sirrah.

Clown. One good woman in ten, madam, which is a
     purifying o' th' song. Would God would serve the
85   world so all the year! We'd find no fault with the
     tithe-woman,° if I were the parson. One in ten,
     quoth 'a!° And° we might have a good woman
     born but or every blazing star, or° at an earth-
     quake, 'twould mend the lottery well; a man may
90   draw his heart out, ere 'a pluck one.

Countess. You'll be gone, sir knave, and do as I com-
     mand you!

Clown. That man should be at woman's command,
     and yet no hurt done! Though honesty be no puri-
95   tan, yet it will do no hurt; it will wear the surplice
     of humility over the black gown of a big heart.°
     I am going, forsooth. The business is for Helen to
     come hither.   *Exit.*

Countess. Well, now.

100 *Steward.* I know, madam, you love your gentlewoman
     entirely.

Countess. Faith, I do. Her father bequeathed her to
     me, and she herself, without other advantage,° may
     lawfully make title to as much love as she finds.

---

77 sentence wise saying   **86 tithe-woman** tenth woman (sent as part
of the tithe, like a tithe-pig)   **87 quoth 'a** says he   **87 And** if
88 or . . . or either . . . or   **95–96 wear . . . heart** i.e., conform
outwardly, masking its pride (the Church of England required the
wearing of the surplice, but clerics inclined toward Calvinism asserted their independence by wearing beneath the surplice the black
Geneva gown)   **103 advantage** interest accruing to a sum of money

There is more owing her than is paid, and more   105
shall be paid her than she'll demand.

Steward. Madam, I was very late° more near her than
I think she wished me. Alone she was, and did
communicate to herself her own words to her own
ears. She thought, I dare vow for her, they touched   110
not any stranger sense.° Her matter was, she loved
your son. Fortune, she said, was no goddess, that
had put such difference betwixt their two estates;
Love no god, that would not extend his might only
where qualities were level; Diana no queen of vir-   115
gins, that would suffer her poor knight° surprised
without rescue in the first assault or ransom after-
ward. This she delivered in the most bitter touch
of sorrow that e'er I heard virgin exclaim in, which
I held my duty speedily to acquaint you withal,   120
sithence° in the loss that may happen it concerns
you something to know it.

Countess. You have discharged this honestly; keep it
to yourself. Many likelihoods informed me of this
before, which hung so tott'ring in the balance that   125
I could neither believe nor misdoubt. Pray you
leave me. Stall this° in your bosom, and I thank
you for your honest care. I will speak with you
further anon.   *Exit Steward.*

Enter Helena.

[*Aside*] Even so it was with me, when I was young;   130
If ever we are nature's, these° are ours; this thorn
Doth to our rose of youth rightly belong;
Our blood° to us, this to our blood is born.
It is the show and seal of nature's truth,
Where love's strong passion is impressed in youth.   135
By our remembrances of days foregone,

---

107 **late** lately   110–11 **touched not any stranger sense** reached
no stranger's ear   116 **knight** i.e., chaste follower of Diana
121 **sithence** since   127 **Stall this** keep this enclosed   131 **these**
sorrows (?) passions (?)   133 **blood** passion (?) disposition (?)

Such were our faults, or then we thought them
    none.
Her eye is sick on't; I observe her now.

Helena. What is your pleasure, madam?

Countess.   You know, Helen,
140 I am a mother to you.

Helena. Mine honorable mistress.

Countess.   Nay, a mother.
Why not a mother? When I said "a mother"
Methought you saw a serpent. What's in "mother"
That you start at it? I say I am your mother,
145 And put you in the catalogue of those
That were enwombèd mine. 'Tis often seen
Adoption strives with nature, and choice breeds
A native slip to us from foreign seeds.°
You ne'er oppressed me with a mother's groan,
150 Yet I express to you a mother's care.
God's mercy, maiden, does it curd thy blood
To say I am thy mother? What's the matter,
That this distempered° messenger of wet,
The many-colored Iris,° rounds thine eye?
Why, that you are my daughter?

155 *Helena.*   That I am not.°

Countess. I say I am your mother.

Helena.   Pardon, madam;
The Count Rousillon cannot be my brother.
I am from humble, he from honored name;
No note upon my parents, his all noble.
160 My master, my dear lord he is, and I
His servant live, and will his vassal die.
He must not be my brother.

147–48 **choice . . . seeds** i.e., a slip that is chosen for grafting from
foreign stock becomes native to us   153 **distempered** disturbed
154 **many-colored Iris** i.e., teardrop (Iris was goddess of the rainbow)
155 **That I am not** (Helena plays on the sense "daughter-in-law")

Countess.   Nor I your mother?

Helena. You are my mother, madam; would you
    were—
  So that my lord, your son, were not my brother—
  Indeed my mother! Or were you both our mothers   165
  I care no more for than I do for heaven,
  So I were not his sister. Can't no other°
  But, I your daughter, he must be my brother?

Countess. Yes, Helen, you might be my daughter-in-
    law.
  God shield° you mean it not! "Daughter" and
    "mother"   170
  So strive upon your pulse! What, pale again?
  My fear hath catched your fondness!° Now I see
  The myst'ry of your loneliness, and find
  Your salt tears' head.° Now to all sense 'tis gross:°
  You love my son! Invention is ashamed   175
  Against the proclamation of thy passion,
  To say thou dost not. Therefore tell me true;
  But tell me then, 'tis so; for look, thy cheeks
  Confess it, t' one to th' other, and thine eyes
  See it so grossly shown in thy behaviors,   180
  That in their kind° they speak it; only sin
  And hellish obstinacy tie thy tongue,
  That truth should be suspected. Speak, is't so?
  If it be so, you have wound a goodly clew;°
  If it be not, forswear't; howe'er, I charge thee, 185
  As heaven shall work in me for thine avail,
  To tell me truly.

Helena.   Good madam, pardon me!

Countess. Do you love my son?

Helena.   Your pardon, noble mistress!

Countess. Love you my son?

---

167 **Can't no other** can it not be otherwise   170 **shield** forbid
172 **fondness** foolishness   174 **head** source   174 **gross** obvious
181 **in their kind** according to their nature, i.e., with tears   184 **clew**
ball of string

Helena.   Do not you love him, madam?

190 *Countess.* Go not about; my love hath in't a bond
    Whereof the world takes note. Come, come, dis-
        close
    The state of your affection, for your passions
    Have to the full appeached.°

Helena.   Then I confess,
    Here on my knee, before high heaven and you,
195 That before you, and next unto high heaven,
    I love your son.
    My friends° were poor but honest; so's my love.
    Be not offended, for it hurts not him
    That he is loved of me; I follow him not
200 By any token of presumptuous suit,
    Nor would I have him till I do deserve him;
    Yet never know how that desert should be.
    I know I love in vain, strive against hope;
    Yet, in this captious° and inteemable° sieve,
205 I still pour in the waters of my love,
    And lack not to lose still.° Thus, Indian-like,
    Religious in mine error, I adore
    The sun that looks upon his worshipper
    But knows of him no more. My dearest madam,
210 Let not your hate encounter with my love
    For loving where you do; but if yourself,
    Whose agèd honor cites° a virtuous youth,
    Did ever, in so true a flame of liking,
    Wish chastely, and love dearly that your Dian
215 Was both herself and Love, O, then give pity
    To her whose state is such that cannot choose
    But lend and give where she is sure to lose;
    That seeks not to find that° her search implies,
    But, riddle-like, lives° sweetly where she dies.

193 **appeached** accused 197 **friends** relatives 204 **captious** (1)
capacious (2) deceitful 204 **inteemable** incapable of pouring forth
(the sieve is capacious enough to accept all the love poured into it,
but is deceptive because it cannot pour forth love) 206 **lack not
to lose still** (1) fail not to go on losing (2) lack not a supply to go on
losing 212 **cites** demonstrates 218 **that** what 219 **lives** i.e., stays
in one place

Countess. Had you not lately an intent—speak truly— *220*
  To go to Paris?

Helena.   Madam, I had.

Countess.   Wherefore? Tell true.

Helena. I will tell truth, by grace itself, I swear.
  You know my father left me some prescriptions
  Of rare and proved effects, such as his reading
  And manifest experience had collected *225*
  For general sovereignty;° and that he willed me
  In heedfull'st reservation° to bestow them,
  As notes whose faculties inclusive were
  More than they were in note.° Amongst the rest,
  There is a remedy, approved,° set down, *230*
  To cure the desperate languishings whereof
  The King is rendered lost.

Countess.   This was your motive
  For Paris, was it? Speak.

Helena. My lord your son made me to think of this;
  Else Paris, and the medicine, and the King, *235*
  Had from the conversation of my thoughts
  Haply been absent then.

Countess.   But think you, Helen,
  If you should tender your supposèd aid,
  He would receive it? He and his physicians
  Are of a mind; he, that they cannot help him; *240*
  They, that they cannot help. How shall they credit
  A poor unlearnèd virgin, when the schools,
  Emboweled° of their doctrine, have left off
  The danger to itself?

Helena.   There's something in't
  More than my father's skill, which was the great'st *245*

---

226 **general sovereignty** universal excellence   227 **In heedfull'st
reservation** i.e. sparingly   228-29 **notes . . . in note** i.e., prescriptions
("notes") more powerful in fact than they were reported ("in note")
to be   230 **approved** tested   243 **Emboweled of their doctrine**
emptied of their knowledge

Of his profession, that his good receipt
Shall for my legacy be sanctified
By th' luckiest stars in heaven; and would your
   honor
But give me leave to try success,° I'd venture
250   The well-lost life of mine on his Grace's cure
By such a day, an hour.

Countess.   Dost thou believe't?

Helena. Ay, madam, knowingly.

Countess. Why, Helen, thou shalt have my leave and
   love,
Means and attendants, and my loving greetings
255   To those of mine in court. I'll stay at home
And pray God's blessing into thy attempt.
Be gone tomorrow; and be sure of this,
What I can help thee to, thou shalt not miss.
                              Exeunt.

249 **try success** test the outcome

ACT II

[Scene I. *Paris. The King's palace.*]

*Enter the King with divers young Lords taking
leave for the Florentine war; Bertram and
Parolles; [Attendants]. Flourish cornets.*

King. Farewell, young lords! These warlike principles
    Do not throw from you; and you, my lords, fare-
      well!
    Share the advice betwixt you; if both gain all,
    The gift doth stretch itself as 'tis received,
    And is enough for both.

First Lord.   'Tis our hope, sir,   5
    After well-ent'red soldiers,° to return
    And find your Grace in health.

King. No, no, it cannot be; and yet my heart
    Will not confess he owes° the malady
    That doth my life besiege. Farewell, young lords!   10
    Whether I live or die, be you the sons

II.i.6 **After well-ent'red soldiers** after becoming experienced soldiers
9 **owes** owns

Of worthy Frenchmen: let higher Italy—
Those bated that inherit but the fall
Of the last monarchy°—see that you come
15 Not to woo honor, but to wed it, when
The bravest questant° shrinks: find what you seek,
That fame may cry you loud. I say, farewell.

First Lord. Health, at your bidding, serve your
    Majesty!

King. Those girls of Italy, take heed of them.
20 They say our French lack language to deny
If they demand; beware of being captives
Before you serve.

Both Lords.   Our hearts receive your warnings.

King. Farewell. [*To attendants*] Come hither to me.
                        [*Exit with Attendants.*]

First Lord. O my sweet lord, that you will stay behind
    us!

Parolles. 'Tis not his fault, the spark.

25 *Second Lord.*   O, 'tis brave wars!

Parolles. Most admirable! I have seen those wars.

Bertram. I am commanded here,° and kept a coil° with
"Too young," and "the next year," and " 'tis too
    early."

Parolles. And° thy mind stand to't, boy, steal away
    bravely.

30 *Bertram.* I shall stay here the forehorse to a smock,°
Creaking my shoes on the plain masonry,
Till honor be bought up, and no sword worn
But one to dance with! By heaven, I'll steal away.

13–14 **Those . . . monarchy** except for those who gain by the fall of
the monarchy (?) except for those who continue in the decadent ways
of the past (?)   16 **questant** seeker   27 **commanded here** ordered
to stay here   27 **kept a coil** bothered   29 **And** if   30 **the forehorse
to a smock** i.e., in the service of women ("forehorse"=leader in a
team of horses)

First Lord. There's honor in the theft.

Parolles.   Commit it, Count.

Second Lord. I am your accessary; and so farewell.   *35*

Bertram. I grow to you, and our parting is a tortured
body.

First Lord. Farewell, Captain.

Second Lord. Sweet Monsieur Parolles!

Parolles. Noble heroes, my sword and yours are kin.   *40*
Good sparks and lustrous, a word, good metals.°
You shall find in the regiment of the Spinii one
Captain Spurio,° with his cicatrice,° an emblem of
war, here on his sinister° cheek; it was this very
sword entrenched it. Say to him I live, and observe   *45*
his reports for me.

First Lord. We shall, noble Captain.   [*Exeunt Lords.*]

Parolles. Mars dote on you for his novices!° [*To
Bertram*] What will ye do?

Bertram. Stay° the King.   *50*

Parolles. Use a more spacious ceremony to the noble
lords; you have restrained yourself within the list°
of too cold an adieu. Be more expressive to them,
for they wear themselves in the cap of the time;
there do muster true gait, eat, speak, and move   *55*
under the influence of the most received° star; and
though the devil lead the measure,° such are to be
followed. After them, and take a more dilated°
farewell.

Bertram. And I will do so.   *60*

41 **metals** (with the additional sense of "mettles," spirits)   43 **Spurio**
(from Italian, "false")   43 **cicatrice** scar   44 **sinister** left   48 **Mars**
. . . **novices** may the god of war watch over you as his pupils
50 **Stay** support   52 **list** boundary (literally the selvage of cloth)
56 **received** fashionable   57 **measure** dance   58 **dilated** extended

Parolles. Worthy fellows, and like to prove most
sinewy sword-men. *Exeunt* [*Bertram and Parolles*].

Enter [*the King and*] *Lafew.*

Lafew. [*Kneeling*] Pardon, my lord, for me and for
my tidings.

King. I'll fee thee to stand up.°

Lafew. [*Rising*] Then here's a man stands that has
65   brought his pardon.
I would you had kneeled, my lord, to ask me mercy,
And that at my bidding you could so stand up.

King. I would I had, so I had broke thy pate°
And asked thee mercy for't.

Lafew.   Good faith, across!°
70   But, my good lord, 'tis thus: will you be cured
Of your infirmity?

King.   No.

Lafew.   O, will you eat
No grapes, my royal fox?° Yes, but you will
My noble grapes, and if my royal fox
Could reach them. I have seen a medicine
75   That's able to breathe life into a stone,
Quicken° a rock, and make you dance canary°
With sprightly fire and motion, whose simple touch
Is powerful to araise King Pippen,° nay,
To give great Charlemain a pen in's hand,
And write to her a love-line.

80 *King.*   What "her" is this?

---

64 **I'll fee thee to stand up** i.e., please arise ("fee"=reward)   68 **pate**
head   69 **across** clumsily (an unskilled tilter might break a lance
"across" instead of head-on)   72 **royal fox** (alluding to Aesop's fox
who said he did not want grapes, when he could not reach them;
Lafew suggests that the King says he does not want to be cured
because he thinks he cannot be cured)   76 **Quicken** endow with life
76 **canary** a lively dance   78 **Pippen** Pepin (died 768)

Lafew. Why, Doctor She! My lord, there's one ar-
   rived,
   If you will see her. Now, by my faith and honor,
   If seriously I may convey my thoughts
   In this my light deliverance,° I have spoke
   With one that, in her sex, her years, profession,°   85
   Wisdom and constancy, hath amazed me more
   Than I dare blame my weakness. Will you see her,
   For that is her demand, and know her business?
   That done, laugh well at me.

King.   Now, good Lafew,
   Bring in the admiration,° that we with thee   90
   May spend our wonder too, or take off thine
   By wond'ring how thou took'st it.

Lafew.   Nay, I'll fit° you,
   And not be all day neither.   [*Goes to door.*]

King. Thus he his special nothing ever prologues.

Lafew. Nay, come your ways.

                Enter Helena.

King.   This haste hath wings indeed.   95

Lafew. Nay, come your ways!
   This is his Majesty; say your mind to him.
   A traitor you do look like, but such traitors
   His Majesty seldom fears. I am Cressid's uncle,°
   That dare leave two together. Fare you well.   *Exit.*   100

King. Now, fair one, does your business follow us?

Helena. Ay, my good lord.
   Gerard de Narbon was my father;
   In what he did profess, well found.°

King.   I knew him.

---

84 **light deliverance** jesting utterance   85 **profession** claims   90 **admiration** wonder   92 **fit** satisfy   99 **Cressid's uncle** Pandarus (who
served as go-between for his niece and Troilus)   104 **well found**
found to be skilled

Helena. The rather will I spare my praises towards
105   him;
        Knowing him is enough. On's bed of death
        Many receipts he gave me, chiefly one,
        Which as the dearest issue of his practice
        And of his old experience th' only darling,
110   He bade me store up as a triple° eye,
        Safer than mine own two; more dear I have so,
        And, hearing your high Majesty is touched
        With that malignant cause wherein the honor
        Of my dear father's gift stands chief in power,
115   I come to tender° it and my appliance,°
        With all bound humbleness.

King.   We thank you, maiden,
        But may not be so credulous of cure,
        When our most learnèd doctors leave us, and
        The congregated College° have concluded
120   That laboring art° can never ransom nature
        From her inaidable estate. I say we must not
        So stain our judgment or corrupt our hope,
        To prostitute our past-cure malady
        To empirics,° or to dissever so
125   Our great self and our credit,° to esteem
        A senseless help, when help past sense we deem.

Helena. My duty then shall pay me for my pains.
        I will no more enforce mine office on you,
        Humbly entreating from your royal thoughts
130   A modest one to bear me back again.

King. I cannot give thee less, to be called grateful.
        Thou thought'st to help me, and such thanks I give
        As one near death to those that wish him live.
        But what at full I know, thou know'st no part,
135   I knowing all my peril, thou no art.

---

110 **triple** third, i.e., the remedy was as valuable as her eyes
115 **tender** offer   115 **appliance** (1) service (2) application, treatment
119 **congregated College** assembled College of Physicians   120 **art**
human skill   124 **empirics** quacks   125 **credit** reputation

Helena. What I can do can do no hurt to try,
　　Since you set up your rest° 'gainst remedy:
　　He that of greatest works is finisher,
　　Oft does them by the weakest minister.
　　So holy writ in babes hath judgment shown,　　140
　　When judges have been babes; great floods have
　　　flown
　　From simple sources; and great seas have dried
　　When miracles have by the great'st° been denied.
　　Oft expectation fails, and most oft there
　　Where most it promises, and oft it hits　　145
　　Where hope is coldest and despair most sits.

King. I must not hear thee; fare thee well, kind maid.
　　Thy pains not used must by thyself be paid.
　　Proffers not took reap thanks for their reward.

Helena. Inspirèd merit so by breath° is barred.　　150
　　It is not so with Him that all things knows,
　　As 'tis with us that square our guess by shows;°
　　But most it is presumption in us when
　　The help of heaven we count the act of men.
　　Dear sir, to my endeavors give consent;　　155
　　Of heaven, not me, make an experiment.
　　I am not an impostor, that proclaim
　　Myself against the level of mine aim,°
　　But know I think, and think I know most sure,
　　My art is not past power, nor you past cure.　　160

King. Art thou so confident? Within what space
　　Hop'st thou my cure?

Helena.　　　　　The greatest grace lending grace,
　　Ere twice the horses of the sun shall bring
　　Their fiery torcher his diurnal ring,°

---

137 **set up your rest** stake all (gambling term)　143 **the great'st** (if
Helena has been thinking of the Red Sea, "the great'st"=Pharaoh)
150 **breath** i.e., your words (contrast to God's breathing into Helen
is implicit in "inspirèd")　152 **square our guess by shows** make decisions by appearances　157–58 **that proclaim . . . aim** i.e., although I announce I will hit the target even before I take aim
164 **diurnal ring** daily circuit

165   Ere twice in murk and occidental damp°
       Moist Hesperus° hath quenched her sleepy lamp,
       Or four and twenty times the pilot's glass°
       Hath told the thievish minutes how they pass,
       What is infirm from your sound parts shall fly,
170   Health shall live free, and sickness freely die.

King. Upon thy certainty and confidence
       What dar'st thou venture?

Helena.   Tax° of impudence,
       A strumpet's boldness, a divulgèd shame,
       Traduced by odious ballads; my maiden's name
175   Seared° otherwise; ne° worse of worst, extended°
       With vilest torture, let my life be ended.

King. Methinks in thee some blessèd spirit doth speak
       His powerful sound within an organ weak;
       And what impossibility would slay
180   In common sense, sense saves another way.
       Thy life is dear, for all that life can rate
       Worth name of life in thee hath estimate:°
       Youth, beauty, wisdom, courage, all
       That happiness and prime° can happy call.
185   Thou this to hazard needs must intimate
       Skill infinite or monstrous desperate.
       Sweet practicer, thy physic° I will try,
       That ministers thine own death if I die.

Helena. If I break time, or flinch in property°
190   Of what I spoke, unpitied let me die,
       And well deserved. Not helping, death's my fee,
       But if I help what do you promise me?

King. Make thy demand.

Helena.   But will you make it even?°

---

165 **occidental damp** (alluding to the sun's alleged setting in the
ocean) 166 **Hesperus** the evening star 167 **glass** hourglass 172
Tax accusation 175 **Seared** branded 175 **ne** nor 175 **extended**
stretched (on the rack) 182 **estimate** value 184 **prime** springtime
(of life), i.e., youth 187 **physic** medicine 189 **flinch in property**
i.e., fail in any detail 193 **make it even** fulfill it

King. Ay, by my scepter and my hopes of heaven.

Helena. Then shalt thou give me with thy kingly hand   *195*
  What husband in thy power I will command:
  Exempted be from me the arrogance
  To choose from forth the royal blood of France
  My low and humble name to propagate
  With any branch or image of thy state;   *200*
  But such a one, thy vassal, whom I know
  Is free for me to ask, thee to bestow.

King. Here is my hand; the premises observed,
  Thy will by my performance shall be served;
  So make the choice of thy own time, for I,   *205*
  Thy resolved patient, on thee still rely.
  More should I question thee, and more I must,
  Though more to know could not be more to trust;
  From whence thou cam'st, how tended on—but rest
  Unquestioned, welcome, and undoubted blest.   *210*
  Give me some help here, ho! If thou proceed
  As high as word, my deed shall match thy deed.
          Flourish. Exit [King with Helena].

[Scene II. *Rousillon. The Count's palace.*]

Enter Countess and Clown.

Countess. Come on, sir. I shall now put you to the
  height of° your breeding.

Clown. I will show myself highly fed and lowly taught.
  I know my business is but to the court.

II.ii.1–2 **put you to the height of** test

5 *Countess.* To the court! Why, what place make you
  special, when you put off that with such contempt?
  "But to the court!"

Clown. Truly, madam, if God have lent a man any
  manners, he may easily put it off at court. He that
10 cannot make a leg,° put off's cap, kiss his hand, and
  say nothing, has neither leg, hands, lip, nor cap;
  and indeed such a fellow, to say precisely, were not
  for the court. But for me, I have an answer will
  serve all men.

15 *Countess.* Marry, that's a bountiful answer that fits
  all questions.

Clown. It is like a barber's chair that fits all buttocks:
  the pin-buttock, the quatch-buttock,° the brawn-
  buttock, or any buttock.

20 *Countess.* Will your answer serve fit to all questions?

Clown. As fit as ten groats° is for the hand of an
  attorney, as your French crown° for your taffety
  punk,° as Tib's rush° for Tom's forefinger, as a
  pancake for Shrove Tuesday,° a morris° for May-
25 day, as the nail to his hole, the cuckold to his horn,
  as a scolding quean° to a wrangling knave, as the
  nun's lip to the friar's mouth; nay, as the pudding°
  to his skin.

Countess. Have you, I say, an answer of such fitness
30 for all questions?

Clown. From below your duke to beneath your constable, it will fit any question.

---

10 **make a leg** make obeisance (by drawing back one leg and bending
the other)   18 **quatch-buttock** fat behind   21 **ten groats** (a groat was
worth fourpence; ten groats was the usual attorney's fee)   22 **French
crown** (1) coin (2) bald or scabby head (caused by syphilis, "the
French disease")   22–23 **taffety punk** finely dressed prostitute
23 **rush** ring made of rush (used in mock weddings)   24 **Shrove
Tuesday** day preceding Ash Wednesday, hence a day of feasting
immediately before Lent   24 **morris** country dance   26 **quean**
prostitute   27 **pudding** sausage

Countess. It must be an answer of most monstrous size
that must fit all demands.

Clown. But a trifle neither,° in good faith, if the   *35*
learned should speak truth of it. Here it is, and all
that belongs to't. Ask me if I am a courtier; it shall
do you no harm to learn.

Countess. To be young again, if we could, I will be
a fool in question, hoping to be the wiser by your   *40*
answer. I pray you, sir, are you a courtier?

Clown. O Lord, sir!° There's a simple putting off.
More, more, a hundred of them.

Countess. Sir, I am a poor friend of yours, that loves
you.
                                                      45
Clown. O Lord, sir! Thick,° thick! Spare not me.

Countess. I think, sir, you can eat none of this homely
meat.

Clown. O Lord, sir! Nay, put me to't, I warrant you.

Countess. You were lately whipped, sir, as I think.   *50*

Clown. O Lord, sir! Spare not me.

Countess. Do you cry, "O Lord, sir!" at your whipping, and "spare not me"? Indeed, your "O Lord,
sir!" is very sequent to° your whipping; you would
answer very well to a whipping, if you were but   *55*
bound to't.°

Clown. I ne'er had worse luck in my life in my "O
Lord, sir!" I see things may serve long, but not
serve ever.

Countess. I play the noble housewife with the time,   *60*
To entertain it so merrily with a fool.

35 **neither** indeed (negating the Countess' conjecture)   42 **O Lord,
sir** (a phrase associated with courtiers)   46 **Thick** quickly   54 **is
very sequent to** i.e., would quickly follow   56 **bound to't** (1) bound
by oath to answer (2) tied to a whipping post

Clown. O Lord, sir! Why, there't serves well again.

Countess. An end, sir! To your business: give Helen
    this,
    And urge her to a present° answer back.
65   Commend me to my kinsmen and my son.
    This is not much.

Clown. Not much commendation to them?

Countess. Not much employment for you. You under-
    stand me?

70   *Clown.* Most fruitfully.° I am there before my legs.

Countess. Haste you again.   *Exeunt.*

[Scene III. *Paris. The King's palace.*]

Enter Bertram, Lafew, and Parolles.

Lafew. They say miracles are past, and we have our
    philosophical persons, to make modern° and famil-
    iar, things supernatural and causeless. Hence is it
    that we make trifles of terrors, ensconcing° our-
5   selves into seeming knowledge, when we should sub-
    mit ourselves to an unknown fear.°

Parolles. Why, 'tis the rarest argument of° wonder
    that hath shot out in our latter times.

Bertram. And so 'tis.

64 **present** immediate   70 **fruitfully** (perhaps a bawdy punning reply, if "understand" means "have intercourse with")   II.iii.2
modern commonplace   4 **ensconcing** fortifying   6 **unknown fear**
i.e., inexplicable mystery   7 **argument of** subject for

Lafew. To be relinquished of the artists—°   10

Parolles. So I say—both of Galen and Paracelsus.°

Lafew. Of all the learned and authentic fellows—

Parolles. Right; so I say.

Lafew. That gave him out incurable—

Parolles. Why, there 'tis; so say I too.   15

Lafew. Not to be helped—

Parolles. Right, as 'twere a man assured of a—

Lafew. Uncertain life and sure death.

Parolles. Just; you say well. So would I have said.

Lafew. I may truly say it is a novelty to the world.   20

Parolles. It is indeed; if you will have it in showing, you shall read it in what-do-ye-call there?

Lafew. [*Reading*] "A showing of a heavenly effect in an earthly actor."

Parolles. That's it, I would have said the very same.   25

Lafew. Why, your dolphin is not lustier;° 'fore me,° I speak in respect—

Parolles. Nay, 'tis strange, 'tis very strange; that is the brief and the tedious of it, and he's of a most facinerious° spirit that will not acknowledge it to   30 be the—

Lafew. Very hand of heaven.

Parolles. Ay, so I say.

Lafew. In a most weak—

Parolles. And debile° minister; great power, great   35

---

10 **artists** physicians   11 **Galen . . . Paracelsus** (renowned physicians; the former was a Greek of the second century B.C., the latter a German of the sixteenth century)   26 **lustier** more vigorous   26 **'fore me** on my soul   30 **facinerious** villainous   35 **debile** weak

transcendence, which should indeed give us a further use to be made than alone the recov'ry of the King, as to be—

Lafew. Generally thankful.

Enter King, Helena, and Attendants.

40 *Parolles.* I would have said it. You say well. Here comes the King.

Lafew. Lustig, as the Dutchman° says. I'll like a maid the better whilst I have a tooth in my head. Why, he's able to lead her a coranto.°

45 *Parolles.* Mor du vinager!° Is not this Helen?

Lafew. 'Fore God, I think so.

King. Go, call before me all the lords in court.
                              [*Exit Attendant.*]
Sit, my preserver, by thy patient's side,
And with this healthful hand, whose banished sense
50 Thou hast repealed,° a second time receive
The confirmation of my promised gift,
Which but attends thy naming.

Enter three or four Lords.

Fair maid, send forth thine eye. This youthful parcel
Of noble bachelors stand at my bestowing,
55 O'er whom both sovereign power and father's voice
I have to use. Thy frank election° make;
Thou hast power to choose, and they none to forsake.

Helena. To each of you one fair and virtuous mistress
Fall, when Love please! Marry, to each but one!

60 *Lafew.* I'd give bay curtal and his furniture,°

---

42 **Dutchman** German   44 **coranto** lively dance   45 **Mor du vinager** death of vinager (a meaningless pseudo-French oath)   50 **repealed** recalled from banishment   56 **frank election** free choice   60 **bay curtal and his furniture** my bay horse with the docked tail, and his trappings

My mouth no more were broken° than these boys',
And writ° as little beard.

King.   Peruse them well:
Not one of those but had a noble father.

Helena. (She addresses her to a lord.) Gentlemen,
Heaven hath through me restored the King to
health.   65

All. We understand it, and thank heaven for you.

Helena. I am a simple maid, and therein wealthiest
That I protest I simply am a maid.
Please it your Majesty, I have done already.
The blushes in my cheeks thus whisper me,   70
"We blush that thou shouldst choose; but, be re-
fused,
Let the white death sit on thy cheek forever,
We'll ne'er come there again."

King.   Make choice and see,
Who shuns thy love shuns all his love in me.

Helena. Now, Dian, from thy altar do I fly,   75
And to imperial Love, that god most high,
Do my sighs stream. [*To First Lord*] Sir, will you
hear my suit?

First Lord. And grant it.

Helena.   Thanks, sir; all the rest is mute.

Lafew. I had rather be in this choice than throw ames-
ace° for my life.   80

Helena. [*To Second Lord*] The honor, sir, that flames
in your fair eyes,
Before I speak, too threat'ningly replies.
Love make your fortunes twenty times above
Her that so wishes and her humble love!

---

61 broken broken to the bit, i.e., tamed (?) missing some teeth (?)
62 writ claimed (?)   **79–80 ames-ace** two aces, the lowest throw in
dicing (the line is ironical, as one might say I would rather be in
this lottery than at death's door)

Second Lord. No better, if you please.

85 *Helena*.   My wish receive,
       Which great Love grant; and so, I take my leave.

Lafew. Do all they deny her?° And they were sons of
       mine, I'd have them whipped, or I would send them
       to th' Turk to make eunuchs of.

Helena. [*To Third Lord*] Be not afraid that I your
90   hand should take,
       I'll never do you wrong, for your own sake.
       Blessing upon your vows, and in your bed
       Find fairer fortune if you ever wed!

Lafew. These boys are boys of ice, they'll none have
95   her. Sure they are bastards to the English; the
       French ne'er got° 'em.

Helena. [*To Fourth Lord*]. You are too young, too
       happy, and too good,
       To make yourself a son out of my blood.

Fourth Lord. Fair one, I think not so.

100 *Lafew*. There's one grape yet. I am sure thy father
       drunk wine.° But if thou be'st not an ass, I am a
       youth of fourteen; I have known thee already.

Helena. [*To Bertram*] I dare not say I take you, but
       I give
       Me and my service, ever whilst I live,
105   Into your guiding power. This is the man.

King. Why then, young Bertram, take her, she's thy
       wife.

Bertram. My wife, my liege? I shall beseech your
       Highness,
       In such a business give me leave to use
       The help of mine own eyes.

---

87 **deny her** (Lafew, at a distance, does not understand that Helena
denies the men) 96 **got** begot 101 **drunk wine** i.e., was manly

King.   Know'st thou not, Bertram,
  What she has done for me?

Bertram.   Yes, my good lord;   110
  But never hope to know why I should marry her.

King. Thou know'st she has raised me from my sickly
  bed.

Bertram. But follows it, my lord, to bring me down
  Must answer for your raising? I know her well;
  She had her breeding° at my father's charge: 115
  A poor physician's daughter my wife! Disdain
  Rather corrupt me ever!°

King. 'Tis only title thou disdain'st in her, the which
  I can build up. Strange is it that our bloods,
  Of color, weight, and heat, poured all together,   120
  Would quite confound distinction, yet stands off
  In differences so mighty. If she be
  All that is virtuous, save what thou dislik'st—
  A poor physician's daughter—thou dislik'st
  Of virtue for the name. But do not so: 125
  From lowest place when virtuous things proceed,
  The place is dignified by th' doer's deed.
  Where great additions swell's° and virtue none,
  It is a dropsied honor. Good alone
  Is good, without a name; vileness is so: 130
  The property° by what it is should go,
  Not by the title. She is young, wise, fair;
  In these to nature she's immediate heir;
  And these breed honor. That is honor's scorn
  Which challenges itself as honor's born°   135
  And is not like the sire. Honors thrive
  When rather from our acts we them derive
  Than our foregoers. The mere word's a slave,
  Deboshed° on every tomb, on every grave

---

115 breeding upbringing   **116–17 Disdain . . . ever** may my disdain
of her ruin me forever   **128 additions swell's** titles inflate us
131 property quality (here, "good" or "vileness")   **135 challenges
. . . born** claims honor by descent   **139 Deboshed** debauched,
debased

140   A lying trophy, and as oft is dumb
Where dust and damned oblivion is the tomb
Of honored bones indeed. What should be said?
If thou canst like this creature as a maid,
I can create the rest. Virtue and she
145   Is her own dower; honor and wealth from me.

Bertram. I cannot love her, nor will strive to do't.

King. Thou wrong'st thyself, if thou shouldst strive to
    choose.

Helena. That you are well restored, my lord, I'm glad;
    Let the rest go.

150 *King.* My honor's at the stake,° which to defeat,
I must produce my power. Here, take her hand,
Proud, scornful boy, unworthy this good gift,
That dost in vile misprision° shackle up
My love and her desert; that canst not dream
155   We, poising us in her defective scale,
Shall weigh thee to the beam;° that wilt not know,
It is in us to plant thine honor where
We please to have it grow. Check thy contempt;
Obey our will, which travails in thy good;
160   Believe not thy disdain, but presently°
Do thine own fortunes that obedient right
Which both thy duty owes and our power claims;
Or I will throw thee from my care forever
Into the staggers° and the careless lapse
165   Of youth and ignorance; both my revenge and hate,
Loosing upon thee in the name of justice,
Without all terms of pity. Speak. Thine answer.

Bertram. Pardon, my gracious lord; for I submit
    My fancy° to your eyes. When I consider
170   What great creation and what dole° of honor

150 **at the stake** (the figure is from bearbaiting; a bear was tied to
a stake, and dogs were set upon him)   153 **misprision** contempt
(with pun on false imprisonment)   155–56 **We . . . beam** i.e., my
(royal "we") word added to Helena will outweigh your objection
160 **presently** immediately   164 **staggers** giddiness (disease of ani-
mals)   169 **fancy** love   170 **dole** portion

Flies where you bid it, I find that she, which late
Was in my nobler thoughts most base, is now
The praisèd of the King; who, so ennobled,
Is as 'twere born so.

King.   Take her by the hand,
And tell her she is thine; to whom I promise   175
A counterpoise, if not to thy estate,
A balance more replete.°

Bertram.   I take her hand.

King. Good fortune and the favor of the King
Smile upon this contract; whose ceremony
Shall seem expedient° on the now-born brief,°   180
And be performed tónight. The solemn feast
Shall more attend upon the coming space,
Expecting absent friends.° As thou lov'st her,
Thy love's to me religious; else, does err.
                    Exeunt. Parolles and Lafew stay
                    behind, commenting of this wedding.

Lafew. Do you hear, monsieur? A word with you.   185

Parolles. Your pleasure, sir?

Lafew. Your lord and master did well to make his
recantation.

Parolles. Recantation! My lord! My master!

Lafew. Ay; is it not a language I speak?   190

Parolles. A most harsh one, and not to be understood
without bloody succeeding.° My master!

Lafew. Are you companion to the Count Rousillon?

Parolles. To any count, to all counts; to what is man.°

176–77 A counterpoise . . . replete i.e., a reward that, if it does not
equal your estate, will overweigh it (?) 180 expedient swift 180
brief royal edict 181–83 The solemn . . . friends the ceremonious
("solemn") feast shall await ("attend") until absent friends arrive
192 succeeding consequences 194 man manly (but Lafew gives it
another sense, "servingman")

195 *Lafew*. To what is count's man; count's master is of
another style.

Parolles. You are too old, sir; let it satisfy you, you
are too old.

Lafew. I must tell thee, sirrah, I write man; to which
200 title age cannot bring thee.

Parolles. What I dare too well do, I dare not do.

Lafew. I did think thee, for two ordinaries,° to be a
pretty wise fellow; thou didst make tolerable vent°
of thy travel; it might pass. Yet the scarves° and the
205 bannerets about thee did manifoldly dissuade me
from believing thee a vessel of too great a burden.°
I have now found thee;° when I lose thee again I
care not. Yet art thou good for nothing but taking
up, and that thou'rt scarce worth.

210 *Parolles*. Hadst thou not the privilege of antiquity°
upon thee—

Lafew. Do not plunge thyself too far in anger, lest
thou hasten thy trial; which if—Lord have mercy on
thee for a hen! So, my good window of lattice, fare
215 thee well; thy casement I need not open, for I look
through thee. Give me thy hand.

Parolles. My lord, you give me most egregious indignity.

Lafew. Ay, with all my heart, and thou art worthy of
it.

220 *Parolles*. I have not, my lord, deserved it.

Lafew. Yes, good faith, every dram of it, and I will
not bate thee a scruple.°

Parolles. Well, I shall be wiser.

---

202 **ordinaries** tavern meals   203 **vent** free talk   204 **scarves** (military men wore scarves, usually over the shoulder; cp. the modern *fourragère*)   206 **burden** capacity   207 **found thee** found you out   210 **antiquity** old age   222 **bate thee a scruple** i.e., diminish by one drop what I have said of you

Lafew. Ev'n as soon as thou canst, for thou hast to
pull at a smack o' th' contrary.° If ever thou be'st   225
bound in thy scarf and beaten, thou shall find what
it is to be proud of thy bondage. I have a desire to
hold my acquaintance with thee, or rather my
knowledge, that I may say, in the default,° "He is
a man I know."   230

Parolles. My lord, you do me most insupportable
vexation.

Lafew. I would it were hell-pains for thy sake, and
my poor doing eternal; for doing° I am past, as I
will by thee, in what motion age will give me leave.   235
                                                Exit.

Parolles. Well, thou hast a son shall take this disgrace
off me; scurvy, old, filthy, scurvy lord! Well, I must
be patient, there is no fettering of authority. I'll
beat him, by my life, if I can meet him with any
convenience,° and he were double and double a   240
lord. I'll have no more pity of his age than I would
have of—I'll beat him, and if I could but meet
him again.

Enter Lafew.

Lafew. Sirrah, your lord and master's married; there's
news for you; you have a new mistress.   245

Parolles. I most unfeignedly beseech your lordship
to make some reservation of your wrongs. He is
my good lord; whom I serve above is my master.

Lafew. Who? God?

Parolles. Ay, sir.   250

Lafew. The devil it is that's thy master. Why dost
thou garter up thy arms o' this fashion? Dost make
hose of thy sleeves? Do other servants so? Thou

---

225 **pull . . . contrary** i.e., take a good taste of your folly   229 **in
the default** when you fail   234 **doing** (perhaps with the bawdy
meaning, "copulating")   240 **convenience** advantage

wert best set thy lower part where thy nose stands.
255   By mine honor, if I were but two hours younger I'd
beat thee. Methink'st thou art a general offense,
and every man should beat thee. I think thou wast
created for men to breathe° themselves upon thee.

Parolles. This is hard and undeserved measure, my
260   lord.

Lafew. Go to, sir. You were beaten in Italy for pick-
ing a kernel out of a pom'granate. You are a
vagabond and no true traveler. You are more saucy
with lords and honorable personages than the com-
265   mission of your birth and virtue gives you heraldry.
You are not worth another word, else I'd call you
knave. I leave you.   *Exit.*

Enter Bertram.

Parolles. Good, very good, it is so then. Good, very
good, let it be concealed awhile.

270   *Bertram.* Undone and forfeited to cares forever!

Parolles. What's the matter, sweetheart?

Bertram. Although before the solemn priest I have
sworn,
I will not bed her.

Parolles. What, what, sweetheart?

275   *Bertram.* O my Parolles, they have married me!
I'll to the Tuscan wars and never bed her.

Parolles. France is a dog-hole, and it no more merits
The tread of a man's foot; to th' wars!

Bertram. There's letters from my mother; what th'
import is,
280   I know not yet.

Parolles. Ay, that would be known. To th' wars, my
boy, to th' wars!

258 **breathe** exercise

He wears his honor in a box unseen,
That hugs his kicky-wicky° here at home,
Spending his manly marrow in her arms,
Which should sustain the bound and high curvet°   285
Of Mars's fiery steed. To other regions!
France is a stable, we that dwell in't jades;°
Therefore to th' war!

Bertram. It shall be so. I'll send her to my house,
Acquaint my mother with my hate to her,   290
And wherefore I am fled; write to the King
That which I durst not speak. His present gift
Shall furnish me to those Italian fields
Where noble fellows strike. Wars is no strife
To the dark house and the detested wife.   295

Parolles. Will this capriccio° hold in thee, art sure?

Bertram. Go with me to my chamber and advise me.
I'll send her straight away. Tomorrow
I'll to the wars, she to her single sorrow.

Parolles. Why, these balls bound; there's noise in it.
'Tis hard;   300
A young man married is a man that's marred.
Therefore away, and leave her bravely; go.
The King has done you wrong; but hush 'tis so.
                         Exit [with Bertram].

---

283 **kicky-wicky** woman (but apparently an obscene term, perhaps
from French *quelque chose*, "something," a euphemism for pudendum)   285 **curvet** prancing   287 **jades** nags   296 **capriccio** caprice
(an affected Italian word)

[Scene IV. *Paris. The King's Palace.*]

Enter Helena and Clown.

Helena. My mother greets me kindly. Is she well?°

Clown. She is not well, but yet she has her health; she's very merry, but yet she is not well. But thanks be given she's very well and wants nothing i' th'
5 world; but yet she is not well.

Helena. If she be very well what does she ail that she's not very well?

Clown. Truly, she's very well indeed, but for two things.

10 *Helena.* What two things?

Clown. One, that she's not in heaven, whither God send her quickly; the other, that she's in earth, from whence God send her quickly.

Enter Parolles.

Parolles. Bless you, my fortunate lady!

15 *Helena.* I hope, sir, I have your good will to have mine own good fortune.

Parolles. You had my prayers to lead them on, and to keep them on have them still. O, my knave, how does my old lady?

20 *Clown.* So that you had her wrinkles and I her money, I would she did as you say.

Parolles. Why, I say nothing.

II.iv.1 **well** (in his reply, the Clown plays on the Elizabethan euphemism in which the dead are said to be well, i.e., well-off, being in heaven)

Clown. Marry, you are the wiser man; for many a
man's tongue shakes out his master's undoing. To
say nothing, to do nothing, to know nothing, and   25
to have nothing, is to be a great part of your
title°—which is within a very little of nothing.

Parolles. Away, th'art a knave.

Clown. You should have said, sir, "Before a knave
th'art a knave"; that's "Before me,° th'art a   30
knave." This had been truth, sir.

Parolles. Go to, thou art a witty fool; I have found
thee.

Clown. Did you find me in° yourself, sir, or were you
taught to find me? The search, sir, was profitable;   35
and much fool may you find in you, even to the
world's pleasure and the increase of laughter.

Parolles. A good knave, i' faith, and well fed.
　Madam, my lord will go away tonight,
　A very serious business calls on him.   40
　The great prerogative and rite of love,
　Which as your due time claims, he does acknowl-
　　edge,
　But puts it off to a compelled restraint;
　Whose want, and whose delay, is strewed with
　　sweets,
　Which they distil now in the curbèd time,°   45
　To make the coming hour o'erflow with joy,
　And pleasure drown the brim.

Helena.　　　　　　　　　　What's his will else?

Parolles. That you will take your instant leave o' th'
　King,
　And make this haste as your own good proceed-
　　ing,°

---

27 **title** possession   30 **before me** (punning on the sense "on my
soul")   34 **in** by   45 **curbèd time** delay (?) time spent in the con-
fining still (?)   49 **as your own good proceeding** as if it originated
from you

50   Strength'ned with what apology you think
May make it probable need.

Helena.   What more commands he?

Parolles. That, having this obtained, you presently
Attend his further pleasure.

Helena. In everything I wait upon his will.

55 *Parolles.* I shall report it so.   *Exit Parolles.*

Helena. I pray you. Come, sirrah. *Exit [with Clown].*

[Scene V. *Paris. The King's palace.*]

Enter Lafew and Bertram.

Lafew. But I hope your lordship thinks not him a
soldier.

Bertram. Yes, my lord, and of very valiant approof.°

Lafew. You have it from his own deliverance.°

5 *Bertram.* And by other warranted testimony.

Lafew. Then my dial goes not true; I took this lark
for a bunting.°

Bertram. I do assure you, my lord, he is very great in
knowledge, and accordingly valiant.

II.v.3 **very valiant approof** great proven valor **4 deliverance** speech
6–7 took this lark for a bunting i.e., underestimated him

Lafew. I have then sinned against his experience and 10
transgressed against his valor; and my state that
way is dangerous, since I cannot yet find in my
heart to repent. Here he comes. I pray you make
us friends; I will pursue the amity.

Enter Parolles.

Parolles. [*To Bertram*] These things shall be done, sir. 15

Lafew. Pray you, sir, who's his tailor?

Parolles. Sir?

Lafew. O, I know him well. Ay sir, he, sir, 's a good
workman, a very good tailor.

Bertram. [*Aside to Parolles*] Is she gone to the King? 20

Parolles. She is.

Bertram. Will she away tonight?

Parolles. As you'll have her.

Bertram. I have writ my letters, casketed my treasure,
Given order for our horses; and tonight, 25
When I should take possession of the bride,
End ere I do begin.

Lafew. [*Aside*] A good traveler is something at the
latter end of a dinner, but one that lies three thirds
and uses a known truth to pass a thousand noth- 30
ings with, should be once heard and thrice beaten.
[*Aloud*] God save you, Captain.

Bertram. Is there any unkindness between my lord
and you, monsieur?

Parolles. I know not how I have deserved to run into 35
my lord's displeasure.

Lafew. You have made shift° to run into't, boots and
spurs and all, like him that leaped into the custard;

---

37 **made shift** managed

and out of it you'll run again rather than suffer
40   question for your residence.°

Bertram. It may be you have mistaken him, my lord.

Lafew. And shall do so ever, though I took him at's
prayers. Fare you well, my lord, and believe this of
me, there can be no kernel in this light nut; the
45   soul of this man is his clothes. Trust him not in
matter of heavy consequence; I have kept of them
tame° and know their natures. Farewell, monsieur;
I have spoken better of you than you have or will
to deserve at my hand, but we must do good against
50   evil.   [*Exit.*]

Parolles. An idle° lord, I swear.

Bertram. I think not so.

Parolles. Why, do you not know him?

Bertram. Yes, I do know him well, and common
speech
55   Gives him a worthy pass.° Here comes my clog.

Enter Helena.

Helena. I have, sir, as I was commanded from you,
Spoke with the King, and have procured his leave
For present parting; only he desires
Some private speech with you.

Bertram.   I shall obey his will.
60   You must not marvel, Helen, at my course,
Which holds not color with the time,° nor does
The ministration and requirèd office
On my particular. Prepared I was not
For such a business; therefore am I found
65   So much unsettled. This drives me to entreat you
That presently you take your way for home,
And rather muse than ask why I entreat you,

39–40 **suffer question for your residence** put up with questions on
why you are there   46 **kept of them tame** had some of them as pets
51 **idle** foolish   55 **pass** reputation   61 **holds not color with the
time** does not match the situation

For my respects° are better than they seem,
And my appointments° have in them a need
Greater than shows itself at the first view   70
To you that know them not. [*Gives a letter*.] This
    to my mother.
'Twill be two days ere I shall see you, so
I leave you to your wisdom.

Helena.   Sir, I can nothing say
But that I am your most obedient servant.

Bertram. Come, come; no more of that.

Helena.   And ever shall   75
With true observance° seek to eke out that
Wherein toward me my homely stars° have failed
To equal my great fortune.

Bertram.   Let that go:
My haste is very great. Farewell; hie home.

Helena. Pray sir, your pardon.

Bertram.   Well, what would you say?   80

Helena. I am not worthy of the wealth I owe,°
Nor dare I say 'tis mine—and yet it is;
But like a timorous thief most fain would steal
What law does vouch mine own.

Bertram.   What would you have?

Helena. Something, and scarce so much: nothing, in-
    deed.   85
I would not tell you what I would, my lord.
Faith, yes—
Strangers and foes do sunder and not kiss.

Bertram. I pray you, stay not, but in haste to horse.

Helena. I shall not break your bidding, good my
    lord.   90
Where are my other men? Monsieur, farewell.
                                        Exit.

68 **respects** reasons 69 **appointments** purposes 76 **observance**
dutiful service 77 **homely stars** fate of low birth 81 **owe** own

Bertram. Go thou toward home, where I will never
   come
Whilst I can shake my sword or hear the drum.
Away, and for our flight.

Parolles.   Bravely, coragio!°
                                   [*Exeunt.*]

---

94 **coragio** courage (Italian)

ACT III

[Scene I. *Florence. The Duke's palace.*]

*Flourish. Enter the Duke of Florence, the two
Frenchmen, with a troop of Soldiers.*

Duke. So that from point to point now have you
    heard
The fundamental reasons of this war,
Whose great decision hath much blood let forth,
And more thirsts after.

First Lord.   Holy seems the quarrel
Upon your Grace's part; black and fearful   *5*
On the opposer.

Duke. Therefore we marvel much our cousin France
Would in so just a business shut his bosom
Against our borrowing prayers.

Second Lord.   Good my lord,
The reasons of our state I cannot yield,°   *10*

III.i.10 **yield** produce

95

But like a common and an outward man
That the great figure of a council frames
By self-unable motion;° therefore dare not
Say what I think of it, since I have found
15   Myself in my incertain grounds to fail
As often as I guessed.

Duke.   Be it his pleasure.

First Lord. But I am sure the younger of our nature,
That surfeit on° their ease, will day by day
Come here for physic.

Duke.   Welcome shall they be;
20   And all the honors that can fly from us
Shall on them settle. You know your places well;
When better fall, for your avails they fell:°
Tomorrow to the field!   *Flourish; [exeunt].*

[Scene II. *Rousillon. The Count's palace.*]

Enter Countess and Clown.

Countess. It hath happened all as I would have had
it, save that he comes not along with her.

Clown. By my troth,° I take my young lord to be a
very melancholy man.

5   *Countess.* By what observance, I pray you?

13 **self-unable motion** impotent guess   18 **surfeit on** grow sick from
22 **When . . . fell** when better places fall vacant, for you they will
have fallen   III.ii.3 **troth** truth

Clown. Why, he will look upon his boot and sing, mend the ruff and sing, ask questions and sing, pick his teeth and sing. I know a man that had this trick of melancholy sold a goodly manor for a song.

Countess. Let me see what he writes, and when he *10* means to come.   [*Reads a letter.*]

Clown. I have no mind to Isbel, since I was at court. Our old lings° and our Isbels o' th' country are nothing like your old ling and your Isbels o' th' court. The brains of my Cupid's knocked out, and *15* I begin to love as an old man loves money, with no stomach.°

Countess. What have we here?

Clown. E'en that you have there.   *Exit.*

Countess. [*Reads*] *a letter.* "I have sent you a *20* daughter-in-law. She hath recovered the King, and undone me. I have wedded her, not bedded her, and sworn to make the 'not'° eternal. You shall hear I am run away; know it before the report come. If there be breadth enough in the world, I *25* will hold a long distance. My duty to you.
                    Your unfortunate son,
                                Bertram."
This is not well, rash and unbridled boy,
To fly the favors of so good a king,   *30*
To pluck his indignation on thy head
By the misprizing° of a maid too virtuous
For the contempt of empire.

                    Enter Clown.

Clown. O madam, yonder is heavy news within, between two soldiers and my young lady.   *35*

Countess. What is the matter?

Clown. Nay, there is some comfort in the news, some

---

13 **lings** salt cod (but also with the sense of "lecherous men") 17 **stomach** appetite   23 **not** (with pun on "knot," the symbol of marriage)   32 **misprizing** despising

comfort; your son will not be killed so soon as I
thought he would.

40 *Countess.* Why should he be killed?

Clown. So say I, madam, if he run away, as I hear
he does. The danger is in standing to't;° that's the
loss of men, though it be the getting of children.
Here they come will tell you more. For my part,
45 I only hear your son was run away.

Enter Helena and two [French] Gentlemen.

First Lord. Save you, good madam.

Helena. Madam, my lord is gone, forever gone.

Second Lord. Do not say so.

Countess. Think upon patience. Pray you, gentlemen,
50 I have felt so many quirks of joy and grief,
That the first face of neither, on the start,
Can woman me° unto't. Where is my son, I pray
you?

Second Lord. Madam, he's gone to serve the Duke
of Florence.
We met him thitherward, for thence we came,
55 And, after some dispatch in hand at court,
Thither we bend again.

Helena. Look on his letter, madam, here's my passport.°
[*Reads*] "When thou canst get the ring upon my
finger, which never shall come off, and show me a
60 child begotten of thy body that I am father to,
then call me husband; but in such a 'then' I write
a 'never.'" This is a dreadful sentence.

Countess. Brought you this letter, gentlemen?

---

42 **standing to't** (1) standing one's ground (2) having sexual intercourse   52 **woman** me make me weep   57 **passport** license to
wander as a beggar

First Lord. Ay, madam, and for the contents' sake are
   sorry for our pains.   65

Countess. I prithee, lady, have a better cheer.
   If thou engrossest° all the griefs are thine,
   Thou robb'st me of a moiety.° He was my son,
   But I do wash his name out of my blood
   And thou art all my child. Towards Florence is he?   70

Second Lord. Ay, madam.

Countess.   And to be a soldier?

Second Lord. Such is his noble purpose, and, be-
   lieve't,
   The Duke will lay upon him all the honor
   That good convenience° claims.

Countess.   Return you thither?

First Lord. Ay, madam, with the swiftest wing of
   speed.   75

Helena. [*Reads*] "Till I have no wife, I have nothing
   in France."
   'Tis bitter.

Countess.   Find you that there?

Helena.   Ay, madam.

First Lord. 'Tis but the boldness of his hand, haply,°
   which his heart was not consenting to.   80

Countess. Nothing in France, until he have no wife!
   There's nothing here that is too good for him
   But only she, and she deserves a lord
   That twenty such rude boys might tend upon
   And call her, hourly, mistress. Who was with him?   85

First Lord. A servant only, and a gentleman which
   I have sometime known.

Countess. Parolles, was it not?

---

67 **thou engrossest** you monopolize   68 **moiety** share   74 **conveni-**
ence propriety   79 **haply** perhaps

First Lord. Ay, my good lady, he.

Countess. A very tainted fellow, and full of wicked-
90   ness.
    My son corrupts a well-derivèd nature
    With his inducement.°

First Lord.   Indeed, good lady,
    The fellow has a deal of that too much,
    Which holds° him much to have.

95   *Countess.* Y'are welcome, gentlemen.
    I will entreat you, when you see my son,
    To tell him that his sword can never win
    The honor that he loses; more I'll entreat you
    Written to bear along.

Second Lord.   We serve you, madam,
100   In that and all your worthiest affairs.

Countess. Not so, but as we change our courtesies.°
    Will you draw near?   *Exit [with Lords and Clown].*

Helena. "Till I have no wife, I have nothing in
    France."
105   Nothing in France until he has no wife!
    Thou shalt have none, Rousillon,° none in France;
    Then hast thou all again. Poor lord! Is't I
    That chase thee from thy country and expose
    Those tender limbs of thine to the event°
110   Of the none-sparing war? And is it I
    That drive thee from the sportive court, where thou
    Wast shot at with fair eyes, to be the mark
    Of smoky muskets? O you leaden messengers,
    That ride upon the violent speed of fire,
115   Fly with false aim, move the still-piecing° air
    That sings with piercing; do not touch my lord!
    Whoever shoots at him, I set him there.
    Whoever charges on his forward breast,

92 **his inducement** i.e., Parolles' influence   94 **holds** profits   101
Not . . . courtesies no, you may serve me only if I may serve you
(a courteous reply)   106 **Rousillon** Bertram, Count of Rousillon
109 **event** outcome   115 **still-piecing** ever-repairing

I am the caitiff° that do hold him to't.
And though I kill him not I am the cause   *120*
His death was so effected. Better 'twere
I met the ravin° lion when he roared
With sharp constraint of hunger; better 'twere
That all the miseries which nature owes°
Were mine at once. No; come thou home, Rousil-
     lon,   *125*
Whence honor but of danger wins a scar,
As oft it loses all.° I will be gone;
My being here it is that holds thee hence.
Shall I stay here to do't? No, no, although
The air of paradise did fan the house   *130*
And angels officed° all. I will be gone,
That pitiful rumor may report my flight
To consolate thine ear. Come night, end day;
For with the dark, poor thief, I'll steal away.   *Exit.*

[Scene III. *Florence.*]

*Flourish. Enter the Duke of Florence, Bertram,
     Drum and Trumpets, Soldiers, Parolles.*

Duke. The general of our horse thou art, and we,
     Great in our hope, lay° our best love and credence
     Upon thy promising fortune.

---

119 **caitiff** wretch   122 **ravin** ravenous   124 **owes** owns, has   126–
27 **Whence . . . all** from where honor at best gains from danger a
scar, and may lose everything   131 **officed** served   III.iii.2 **lay**
wager

Bertram.   Sir, it is
    A charge too heavy for my strength; but yet
5   We'll strive to bear it for your worthy sake
    To th' extreme edge of hazard.

Duke.   Then go thou forth,
    And fortune play upon thy prosperous helm,°
    As thy auspicious mistress!

Bertram.   This very day,
    Great Mars, I put myself into thy file!
10 Make me but like my thoughts and I shall prove
    A lover of thy drum, hater of love. *Exeunt omnes.*

[Scene IV. *Rousillon. The Count's palace.*]

Enter Countess and Steward.

Countess. Alas! And would you take the letter of her?
    Might you not know she would do as she has done,
    By sending me a letter? Read it again.

[*Steward reads the*] *letter.* "I am Saint Jaques' pilgrim,°
    thither gone.
5   Ambitious love hath so in me offended
    That barefoot plod I the cold ground upon,
    With sainted vow my faults to have amended.
    Write, write, that from the bloody course of war
    My dearest master, your dear son, may hie.°
10 Bless him at home in peace, whilst I from far
    His name with zealous fervor sanctify.

7 **helm** helmet   III.iv.4 **Saint Jaques' pilgrim** making a pilgrimage
to St. James's shrine (at Compostela, in Spain; "Jaques" is disyllabic:
Jă kis)   9 **hie** hurry

His taken° labors bid him me forgive;
I, his despiteful Juno,° sent him forth
From courtly friends with camping foes to live,
Where death and danger dogs the heels of worth.   *15*
He is too good and fair for death and me,
Whom I myself embrace to set him° free."

[*Countess.*] Ah, what sharp stings are in her mild-
    est words!
Rinaldo, you did never lack advice° so much
As letting her pass so; had I spoke with her,   *20*
I could have well diverted her intents,
Which thus she hath prevented.

Steward.   Pardon me, madam.
If I had given you this at overnight,°
She might have been o'erta'en; and yet she writes,
Pursuit would be but vain.

Countess.   What angel shall   *25*
Bless this unworthy husband? He cannot thrive,
Unless her prayers, whom heaven delights to hear
And loves to grant, reprieve him from the wrath
Of greatest justice. Write, write, Rinaldo,
To this unworthy husband of his wife;   *30*
Let every word weigh heavy of her worth
That he does weigh too light. My greatest grief,
Though little he do feel it, set down sharply.
Dispatch the most convenient messenger.
When haply he shall hear that she is gone,   *35*
He will return; and hope I may that she,
Hearing so much, will speed her foot again,
Led hither by pure love. Which of them both
Is dearest to me, I have no skill in sense
To make distinction. Provide this messenger.   *40*
My heart is heavy and mine age is weak;
Grief would have tears, and sorrow bids me speak.
                                    Exeunt.

12 **taken** undertaken   13 **despiteful Juno** (alluding to Juno's per-
secution of Hercules, on whom she imposed the legendary twelve
labors)   17 **Whom . . . him** i.e., Death . . . Bertram   19 **advice**
discretion   23 **at overnight** last night

[Scene V. *Outside Florence.*]

A tucket° afar off. Enter old Widow of Florence,
her daughter [Diana], and Mariana, with other
citizens.

Widow. Nay come, for if they do approach the city,
we shall lose all the sight.

Diana. They say the French count has done most
honorable service.

5 *Widow.* It is reported that he has taken their great'st
commander, and that with his own hand he slew
the Duke's brother. [*Tucket.*] We have lost our
labor; they are gone a contrary way. Hark! You
may know by their trumpets.

10 *Mariana.* Come, let's return again, and suffice ourselves with the report of it. Well, Diana, take heed
of this French earl. The honor of a maid is her
name, and no legacy is so rich as honesty.°

Widow. I have told my neighbor how you have been
15 solicited by a gentleman his companion.

Mariana. I know that knave, hang him, one Parolles;
a filthy officer he is in those suggestions for the
young earl. Beware of them, Diana: their promises,
enticements, oaths, tokens, and all these engines°
20 of lust, are not the things they go under;° many a
maid hath been seduced by them. And the misery
is, example, that so terrible shows in the wrack of
maidenhood, cannot for all that dissuade succes-

III.v.s.d. **tucket** trumpet call heralding the approach of an important
person   13 **honesty** chastity   19 **engines** devices   20 **go under** mas-
querade as

sion,° but that they are limed° with the twigs that
threatens them. I hope I need not to advise you   25
further, but I hope your own grace will keep you
where you are, though there were no further danger
known but the modesty which is so lost.

Diana. You shall not need to fear me.

Enter Helena, [disguised as a pilgrim].

Widow. I hope so. Look, here comes a pilgrim. I   30
know she will lie° at my house; thither they send
one another. I'll question her. God save you, pilgrim! Whither are you bound?

Helena. To Saint Jaques le Grand.
Where do the palmers° lodge, I do beseech you?   35

Widow. At the Saint Francis here beside the port.°

Helena. Is this the way?

Widow. Ay, marry, is't. (*A march afar.*) Hark you!
    They come this way.
If you will tarry, holy pilgrim,
But till the troops come by,
I will conduct you where you shall be lodged;   40
The rather for I think I know your hostess
As ample° as myself.

Helena.   Is it yourself?

Widow. If you shall please so, pilgrim.

Helena. I thank you, and will stay upon your leisure.°   45

Widow. You came, I think, from France?

Helena.   I did so.

Widow. Here you shall see a countryman of yours
    That has done worthy service.

23–24 **dissuade succession** prevent others from following   24 **limed**
caught (as by birdlime, a sticky substance smeared on twigs to trap
birds)   31 **lie** lodge   35 **palmers** pilgrims   36 **port** city gate   43
ample well   45 **stay upon your leisure** wait until convenient for you

Helena.   His name, I pray you.

Diana. The Count Rousillon. Know you such a one?

50 *Helena.* But by the ear, that hears most nobly of him;
    His face I know not.

Diana.   Whatsome'er he is,
    He's bravely taken° here. He stole from France,
    As 'tis reported, for the King had married him
    Against his liking. Think you it is so?

55 *Helena.* Ay, surely, mere° the truth. I know his lady.

Diana. There is a gentleman that serves the Count
    Reports but coarsely of her.

Helena.   What's his name?

Diana. Monsieur Parolles.

Helena.   O, I believe with him,
    In argument of praise, or to the worth
60 Of the great Count himself, she is too mean
    To have her name repeated; all her deserving
    Is a reservèd honesty,° and that
    I have not heard examined.

Diana.   Alas, poor lady!
    'Tis a hard bondage to become the wife
65 Of a detesting lord.

Widow. I warrant, good creature, wheresoe'er she is,
    Her heart weighs sadly. This young maid might do
        her
    A shrewd turn,° if she pleased.

Helena.   How do you mean?
    Maybe the amorous Count solicits her
    In the unlawful purpose.

70 *Widow.*   He does indeed,

---

52 **bravely taken** well esteemed   55 **mere** absolutely   62 **reservèd honesty** preserved chastity   68 **shrewd turn** nasty deed (with sexual implication in "turn")

And brokes° with all that can in such a suit
Corrupt the tender honor of a maid;
But she is armed for him, and keeps her guard
In honestest defense.

Mariana.   The gods forbid else!

*Drum and colors. Enter Bertram, Parolles, and
the whole army.*

Widow. So, now they come.   75
That is Antonio, the Duke's eldest son;
That, Escalus.

Helena.   Which is the Frenchman?

Diana.   He—
That with the plume; 'tis a most gallant fellow.
I would he loved his wife. If he were honester
He were much goodlier. Is't not a handsome gentle-
  man?   80

Helena. I like him well.

Diana. 'Tis pity he is not honest. Yond's that same
  knave
That leads him to these places. Were I his lady
I would poison that vile rascal.

Helena.   Which is he?

Diana. That jackanapes with scarves. Why is he
  melancholy?   85

Helena. Perchance he's hurt i' th' battle.

Parolles. Lose our drum! Well.

Mariana. He's shrewdly° vexed at something. Look,
he has spied us.

Widow. Marry, hang you!   90

Mariana. And your curtsy, for a ring-carrier!°
            Exit [Bertram, with Parolles and the army].

---

71 **brokes** bargains   88 **shrewdly** bitterly   91 **ring-carrier** bawd

Widow. The troop is past. Come, pilgrim, I will bring
    you
  Where you shall host;° of enjoined° penitents
  There's four or five, to great Saint Jaques bound,
  Already at my house.

95 *Helena.*   I humbly thank you.
  Please it this matron and this gentle maid
  To eat with us tonight, the charge and thanking
  Shall be for me; and, to requite you further,
  I will bestow some precepts of° this virgin
  Worthy the note.

100 *Both.*   We'll take your offer kindly.
                             Exeunt.

[Scene VI. *The Florentine camp.*]

*Enter Bertram and the [two] Frenchmen, as at
first.*

First Lord. Nay, good my lord, put him to't;° let him
  have his way.

Second Lord. If your lordship find him not a hilding,°
  hold me no more in your respect.

5 *First Lord.* On my life, my lord, a bubble.

Bertram. Do you think I am so far deceived in him?

First Lord. Believe it, my lord, in mine own direct

---

93 **host** lodge   93 **enjoined** bound by oath   99 **of** on   III.vi.1 **put
him to't** test him   3 **hilding** worthless fellow

knowledge, without any malice, but to speak of him
as my kinsman,° he's a most notable coward, an
infinite and endless liar, an hourly promise-breaker,   10
the owner of no one good quality worthy your lordship's entertainment.°

Second Lord. It were fit you knew him, lest reposing
too far in his virtue which he hath not, he might at
some great and trusty business in a main danger   15
fail you.

Bertram. I would I knew in what particular action to
try him.

Second Lord. None better than to let him fetch off his
drum,° which you hear him so confidently under-   20
take to do.

First Lord. I, with a troop of Florentines, will suddenly surprise him; such I will have whom I am
sure he knows not from the enemy. We will bind
and hoodwink° him so, that he shall suppose no   25
other but that he is carried into the leaguer° of the
adversaries when we bring him to our own tents.
Be but your lordship present at his examination;
if he do not for the promise of his life and in the
highest compulsion of base fear offer to betray you   30
and deliver all the intelligence° in his power against
you, and that with the divine forfeit of his soul
upon oath, never trust my judgment in anything.

Second Lord. O, for the love of laughter, let him fetch
his drum. He says he has a stratagem for't. When   35
your lordship sees the bottom of his success in't,
and to what metal this counterfeit lump of ore will
be melted, if you give him not John Drum's enter-
tainment° your inclining cannot be removed. Here
he comes.   40

9 **as my kinsman** i.e., impartially   12 **entertainment** maintenance
19–20 **fetch off his drum** recapture his drum (the loss of the drum
was a military disgrace)   25 **hoodwink** blindfold   26 **leaguer** camp
31 **intelligence** information   38–39 **John Drum's entertainment**
manhandling

Enter Parolles.

First Lord. O, for the love of laughter, hinder not the
honor of his design; let him fetch off his drum in
any hand.

Bertram. How now, monsieur! This drum sticks sorely
45   in your disposition.

Second Lord. A pox° on't, let it go, 'tis but a drum.

Parolles. "But a drum!" Is't "but a drum"? A drum
so lost! There was excellent command: to charge
in with our horse upon our own wings, and to rend
50   our own soldiers!

Second Lord. That was not to be blamed in the command of the service; it was a disaster of war that
Caesar himself could not have prevented if he had
been there to command.

55   **Bertram.** Well, we cannot greatly condemn our success;° some dishonor we had in the loss of that
drum, but it is not to be recovered.

Parolles. It might have been recovered.

Bertram. It might, but it is not now.

60   **Parolles.** It is to be recovered. But that the merit of
service is seldom attributed to the true and exact
performer, I would have that drum or another, or
hic jacet.°

Bertram. Why, if you have a stomach,° to't, monsieur.
65   If you think your mystery° in stratagem can bring
this instrument of honor again into his native quar-
ter, be magnanimous in the enterprise, and go on;
I will grace the attempt for a worthy exploit. If you
speed° well in it, the Duke shall both speak of it
70   and extend to you what further becomes his great-

---

46 **pox** plague (literally, syphilis)   55–56 **success** outcome, fortune
(either good or bad)   63 **hic jacet** here lies (Latin, beginning an
epitaph)   64 **stomach** appetite   65 **mystery** art, skill   69 **speed**
prosper

ness, even to the utmost syllable of your worthiness.

Parolles. By the hand of a soldier, I will undertake it.

Bertram. But you must not now slumber in it.

Parolles. I'll about it this evening, and I will presently   75
pen down my dilemmas,° encourage myself in my
certainty, put myself into my mortal preparation;°
and by midnight look to hear further from me.

Bertram. May I be bold to acquaint his Grace you
are gone about it?   80

Parolles. I know not what the success will be, my
lord, but the attempt I vow.

Bertram. I know, th'art valiant; and to the possibility° of thy soldiership will subscribe for thee. Farewell.   85

Parolles. I love not many words.   *Exit.*

First Lord. No more than a fish loves water. Is not
this a strange fellow, my lord, that so confidently
seems to undertake this business, which he knows
is not to be done, damns himself to do, and dares   90
better be damned than to do't.

Second Lord. You do not know him, my lord, as we
do. Certain it is that he will steal himself into a
man's favor and for a week escape a great deal of
discoveries, but when you find him out you have   95
him ever after.

Bertram. Why, do you think he will make no deed at
all of this that so seriously he does address himself
unto?

First Lord. None in the world, but return with an in-   100
vention, and clap upon you two or three probable
lies; but we have almost embossed him.° You shall

---

76 **dilemmas** arguments   77 **my mortal preparation** preparation for
my death (?) my weapons for killing (?)   83–84 **possibility** capacity
102 **embossed him** exhausted him (hunting term)

see his fall tonight, for indeed he is not for your
lordship's respect.

105 *Second Lord.* We'll make you some sport with the fox
ere we case° him. He was first smoked° by the old
lord Lafew. When his disguise and he is parted, tell
me what a sprat° you shall find him; which you
shall see this very night.

110 *First Lord.* I must go look my twigs; he shall be
caught.

Bertram. Your brother, he shall go along with me.

First Lord. As't please your lordship: I'll leave you.
Exit.

Bertram. Now will I lead you to the house and show
you
The lass I spoke of.

115 *Second Lord.*   But you say she's honest.

Bertram. That's all the fault. I spoke with her but
once,
And found her wondrous cold, but I sent to her,
By this same coxcomb that we have i' th' wind,°
Tokens and letters which she did re-send,
120 And this is all I have done. She's a fair creature;
Will you go see her?

Second Lord.   With all my heart, my lord.
Exeunt.

106 **case** skin   106 **smoked** exposed (like a fox smoked out)   108
sprat small fish   118 **have i' th' wind** are hunting

[Scene VII. *Florence. The Widow's house.*]

Enter Helena and Widow.

Helena. If you misdoubt me that I am not she,
 I know not how I shall assure you further,
 But I shall lose the grounds I work upon.°

Widow. Though my estate be fall'n, I was well born,
 Nothing acquainted with these businesses,   5
 And would not put my reputation now
 In any staining act.

Helena.   Nor would I wish you.
 First give me trust the Count he is my husband,
 And what to your sworn counsel I have spoken°
 Is so from word to word; and then you cannot,   10
 By the good aid that I of you shall borrow,
 Err in bestowing it.

Widow.   I should believe you,
 For you have showed me that which well approves
 Y'are great in fortune.

Helena.   Take this purse of gold,
 And let me buy your friendly help thus far,   15
 Which I will over-pay and pay again
 When I have found it. The Count he woos your
     daughter,
 Lays down his wanton siege before her beauty,
 Resolved to carry° her; let her in fine° consent
 As we'll direct her how 'tis best to bear it.
 Now his important° blood will nought deny   20
 That she'll demand; a ring the County° wears,

III.vii.3 **But . . . upon** i.e., unless ("But") I reveal myself to Bertram
9 **to . . . spoken** I have confided to you, upon your oath of secrecy
19 **carry** conquer   19 **in fine** finally   21 **important** importunate,
pressing   22 **County** Count

That downward hath succeeded in his house
From son to son some four or five descents
25 Since the first father wore it. This ring he holds
In most rich choice; yet, in his idle fire,
To buy his will° it would not seem too dear,
Howe'er repented after.

Widow.   Now I see
The bottom of your purpose.

30 *Helena.* You see it lawful then. It is no more
But that your daughter, ere she seems as won,
Desires this ring; appoints him an encounter;
In fine, delivers me to fill the time,
. Herself most chastely absent. After,
35 To marry her° I'll add three thousand crowns
To what is passed already.

Widow.   I have yielded.
Instruct my daughter how she shall persever°
That time and place with this deceit so lawful
May prove coherent.° Every night he comes
40 With musics of all sorts, and songs composed
To her unworthiness. It nothing steads° us
To chide him from our eaves, for he persists
As if his life lay on't.

Helena.   Why then tonight
Let us assay our plot, which, if it speed,°
45 Is wicked meaning° in a lawful deed,
And lawful meaning in a lawful act,
Where both not sin, and yet a sinful fact.
But let's about it.   [*Exeunt.*]

---

27 **will** lust   35 **To marry her** i.e., as a dowry to help her marry
37 **persever** (accent on second syllable)   39 **coherent** in accordance
41 **steads** helps   44 **speed** prosper   45 **meaning** intention (the point
of this passage is that Bertram's intention is wicked, though his deed
—copulating with his wife—will be lawful; Helena's intention and
her act will be good, and the deed will not be a sin though in
Bertram's mind he will be sinning)

ACT IV

[Scene I. *Outside the Florentine camp.*]

*Enter one of the Frenchmen, with five or six
other Soldiers in ambush.*

First Lord. He can come no other way but by this
hedge-corner. When you sally upon him, speak
what terrible language you will; though you understand it not yourselves, no matter; for we must not
seem to understand him, unless someone among us   5
whom we must produce for an interpreter.

First Soldier. Good captain, let me be th' interpreter.

First Lord. Art not acquainted with him? Knows he
not thy voice?

First Soldier. No sir, I warrant you.   10

First Lord. But what linsey-woolsey° hast thou to
speak to us again?

IV.i.11 **linsey-woolsey** nonsense (literally a coarse fabric of linen
and wool)

First Soldier. E'en such as you speak to me.

First Lord. He must think us some band of strangers°
15 i' th' adversary's entertainment. Now he hath a
smack of all neighboring languages; therefore we
must everyone be a man of his own fancy, not to
know what we speak one to another; so we seem
to know is to know straight our purpose; choughs'°
20 language, gabble enough and good enough. As for
you, interpreter, you must seem very politic. But
couch, ho! Here he comes to beguile two hours in
a sleep, and then to return and swear the lies he
forges.

Enter Parolles.

25 *Parolles.* Ten o'clock. Within these three hours 'twill
be time enough to go home. What shall I say I have
done? It must be a very plausive° invention that
carries it. They begin to smoke me, and disgraces
have of late knocked too often at my door. I find
30 my tongue is too foolhardy, but my heart hath the
fear of Mars before it and of his creatures, not
daring the reports of my tongue.

First Lord. [*Aside*] This is the first truth that e'er
thine own tongue was guilty of.

35 *Parolles.* What the devil should move me to undertake the recovery of this drum, being not ignorant
of the impossibility, and knowing I had no such
purpose? I must give myself some hurts, and say
I got them in exploit. Yet slight ones will not carry
40 it. They will say, "Came you off with so little?"
And great ones I dare not give. Wherefore, what's
the instance? Tongue, I must put you into a butter-
woman's° mouth, and buy myself another of Bajazet's mule° if you prattle me into these perils.

14 **strangers** foreigners   19 **choughs'** jackdaws'   27 **plausive** plaus-
ible   42–43 **butter-woman's** i.e., shrill-voiced woman's   43–44 **Bajazet's mule** (mules were proverbial for muteness, but "Bajazet" is
inexplicable)

First Lord. [*Aside*] Is it possible he should know what   45
he is, and be that he is?

Parolles. I would the cutting of my garments would
serve the turn, or the breaking of my Spanish sword.

First Lord. [*Aside*] We cannot afford you so.°

Parolles. Or the baring of my beard, and to say it was   50
in stratagem.

First Lord. [*Aside*] 'Twould not do.

Parolles. Or to drown my clothes, and say I was
stripped.

First Lord. [*Aside*] Hardly serve.   55

Parolles. Though I swore I leaped from the window
of the citadel—

First Lord. [*Aside*] How deep?

Parolles. Thirty fathom.

First Lord. [*Aside*] Three great oaths would scarce   60
make that be believed.

Parolles. I would I had any drum of the enemy's; I
would swear I recovered it.

First Lord. [*Aside*] You shall hear one anon.°

Parolles. A drum now of the enemy's—   65
                                       Alarum° within.

First Lord. Throca movousus, cargo, cargo, cargo.

All. Cargo, cargo, cargo, villianda par corbo, cargo.

Parolles. O, ransom, ransom! Do not hide mine eyes.
                                       [*They blindfold him.*]

Interpreter. Boskos thromuldo boskos.

Parolles. I know you are the Muskos' regiment,
And I shall lose my life for want of language.   70

---

49 **afford you so** let you off thus   64 **anon** soon   66 s.d. **Alarum**
call to arms

If there be here German, or Dane, low Dutch,
Italian, or French, let him speak to me,
I'll discover° that which shall undo the Florentine.

75 *Interpreter. Boskos vauvado.* I understand thee, and
can speak thy tongue. *Kerelybonto.* Sir, betake thee
to thy faith, for seventeen poniards are at thy
bosom.

Parolles. O!

80 *Interpreter.* O, pray, pray, pray! *Manka revania
dulche.*

First Lord. Oscorbidulchos volivorco.

Interpreter. The General is content to spare thee yet,
And, hoodwinked as thou art, will lead thee on
85 To gather from thee. Haply thou mayst inform
Something to save thy life.

Parolles.   O, let me live!
And all the secrets of our camp I'll show,
Their force, their purposes; nay, I'll speak that
Which you will wonder at.

Interpreter.   But wilt thou faithfully?

Parolles. If I do not, damn me.

90 *Interpreter.*   *Acordo linta.*
Come on, thou art granted space.
                              Exit [with Parolles guarded].

A short alarum within.°

First Lord. Go, tell the Count Rousillon and my
brother
We have caught the woodcock° and will keep him
muffled
Till we do hear from them.

---

74 **discover** reveal   91 s.d. **A short alarum within** (perhaps Parolles
is taken off to a ruffle of drums)   93 **woodcock** stupid bird

Soldier.   Captain, I will.

First Lord. 'A° will betray us all unto ourselves; in-   95
    form on that.

Soldier. So I will, sir.

First Lord. Till then, I'll keep him dark, and safely
    locked.   *Exit [with the others]*.

[Scene II. *Florence. The Widow's house.*]

Enter Bertram and the maid called Diana.

Bertram. They told me that your name was Fontibell.

Diana. No, my good lord, Diana.

Bertram.   Titled goddess;
    And worth it, with addition.° But, fair soul,
    In your fine frame hath love no quality?
    If the quick fire of youth light not your mind   5
    You are no maiden but a monument.
    When you are dead you should be such a one
    As you are now; for you are cold and stern,
    And now you should be as your mother was
    When your sweet self was got.   10

Diana. She then was honest.

Bertram.   So should you be.

Diana.   No.

95 'A he   IV.ii.3 **addition** further distinguished title

My mother did but duty; such, my lord,
As you owe to your wife.

Bertram.   No more o' that!
I prithee, do not strive against my vows;
15   I was compelled to her, but I love thee
By love's own sweet constraint, and will forever
Do thee all rights of service.

Diana.   Ay, so you serve us
Till we serve you; but when you have our roses,
You barely leave our thorns to prick ourselves,
And mock us with our bareness.

20   *Bertram.*   How have I sworn!

Diana. 'Tis not the many oaths that makes the truth,
But the plain single vow that is vowed true.
What is not holy, that we swear not by,
But take the High'st to witness; then, pray you, tell
me:
25   If I should swear by Jove's great attributes
I loved you dearly, would you believe my oaths
When I did love you ill?° This has no holding,
To swear by Him whom I protest to love
That I will work against Him. Therefore your oaths
30   Are words and poor conditions but unsealed,°
At least in my opinion.

Bertram.   Change it, change it;
Be not so holy-cruel. Love is holy,
And my integrity ne'er knew the crafts
That you do charge men with. Stand no more off,
35   But give thyself unto my sick desires,
Who then recovers. Say thou art mine, and ever
My love as it begins shall so persever.

Diana. I see that men make rope's in such a scarre,°
That we'll forsake ourselves. Give me that ring.

27 **ill** not well, not at all   30 **but unsealed** merely invalid   38 **I see
. . . scarre** (possibly "scarre" means "splice" and thus "snare," but
the text is probably corrupt)

Bertram. I'll lend it thee, my dear, but have no power 40
   To give it from me.

Diana.   Will you not, my lord?

Bertram. It is an honor 'longing to our house,
   Bequeathèd down from many ancestors,
   Which were the greatest obloquy i' th' world
   In me to lose.

Diana.   Mine honor's such a ring; 45
   My chastity's the jewel of our house,
   Bequeathèd down from many ancestors,
   Which were the greatest obloquy i' th' world
   In me to lose. Thus your own proper° wisdom
   Brings in the champion Honor on my part 50
   Against your vain assault.

Bertram.   Here, take my ring.
   My house, mine honor, yea, my life be thine,
   And I'll be bid by thee.

Diana. When midnight comes, knock at my chamber-
     window:
   I'll order take my mother shall not hear. 55
   Now will I charge you in the band° of truth,
   When you have conquered my yet maiden bed,
   Remain there but an hour, nor speak to me.
   My reasons are most strong and you shall know
     them
   When back again this ring shall be delivered; 60
   And on your finger in the night I'll put
   Another ring, that what in time proceeds
   May token to the future our past deeds.
   Adieu till then; then fail not. You have won
   A wife of me, though there my hope be done. 65

Bertram. A heaven on earth I have won by wooing
     thee.
                              [*Exit.*]

Diana. For which live long to thank both heaven and
     me!

---

49 **proper** personal   56 **band** bond

    You may so in the end.
    My mother told me just how he would woo,
70 As if she sat in's heart. She says all men
    Have the like oaths. He had sworn to marry me
    When his wife's dead; therefore I'll lie with him
    When I am buried. Since Frenchmen are so braid,°
    Marry that will, I live and die a maid.
75 Only, in this disguise, I think't no sin
    To cozen° him that would unjustly win.   *Exit.*

[Scene III. *The Florentine camp.*]

*Enter the two French Captains, and some
two or three Soldiers.*

First Lord. You have not given him his mother's
    letter?

Second Lord. I have delivered it an hour since. There
    is something in't that stings his nature, for on the
5   reading it he changed almost into another man.

First Lord. He has much worthy blame laid upon him
    for shaking off so good a wife and so sweet a lady.

Second Lord. Especially he hath incurred the ever-
    lasting displeasure of the King, who had even
10   tuned his bounty to sing happiness to him. I will
    tell you a thing, but you shall let it dwell darkly
    with you.

73 **braid** deceitful (?)   76 **cozen** deceive

First Lord. When you have spoken it, 'tis dead, and I
   am the grave of it.

Second Lord. He hath perverted a young gentlewoman   15
   here in Florence, of a most chaste renown, and this
   night he fleshes his will in the spoil of her honor; he
   hath given her his monumental° ring, and thinks
   himself made in the unchaste composition.°

First Lord. Now, God delay our rebellion! As we are   20
   ourselves, what things are we!

Second Lord. Merely° our own traitors. And as in the
   common course of all treasons we still see them
   reveal themselves till they attain to their abhorred
   ends, so he that in this action contrives against his   25
   own nobility, in his proper° stream o'erflows° himself.

First Lord. Is it not meant damnable in us to be
   trumpeters of our unlawful intents? We shall not
   then have his company tonight?   30

Second Lord. Not till after midnight, for he is dieted°
   to his hour.

First Lord. That approaches apace. I would gladly
   have him see his company anatomized,° that he
   might take a measure of his own judgments, wherein   35
   so curiously he had set this counterfeit.°

Second Lord. We will not meddle with him till he°
   come, for his presence must be the whip of the
   other.

First Lord. In the meantime, what hear you of these   40
   wars?

Second Lord. I hear there is an overture of peace.

IV.iii.18 **monumental** serving as a memento   19 **composition** bargain   22 **Merely** utterly   26 **proper** own   26 **o'erflows** (1) betrays
in talk (2) drowns   31 **dieted** restricted   34 **company anatomized**
companion (i.e., Parolles) minutely analyzed   35–36 **wherein . . .
counterfeit** in which he has so elaborately set this false jewel
37 **him . . . he** i.e., Parolles . . . Bertram

First Lord. Nay, I assure you, a peace concluded.

Second Lord. What will Count Rousillon do then?
45 Will he travel higher, or return again into France?

First Lord. I perceive by this demand you are not
altogether of his council.

Second Lord. Let it be forbid, sir; so should I be a
great deal of his act.

50 *First Lord.* Sir, his wife some two months since fled
from his house. Her pretense° is a pilgrimage to
Saint Jaques le Grand; which holy undertaking with
most austere sanctimony° she accomplished; and,
there residing, the tenderness of her nature became
55 as a prey to her grief; in fine, made a groan of her
last breath, and now she sings in heaven.

Second Lord. How is this justified?°

First Lord. The stronger part of it by her own letters,
which makes her story true even to the point of her
60 death. Her death itself, which could not be her
office to say is come, was faithfully confirmed by the
rector° of the place.

Second Lord. Hath the Count all this intelligence?°

First Lord. Ay, and the particular confirmations, point
65 from point, to the full arming of the verity.

Second Lord. I am heartily sorry that he'll be glad of
this.

First Lord. How mightily sometimes we make us comforts of our losses!

70 *Second Lord.* And how mightily some other times we
drown our gain in tears! The great dignity that his
valor hath here acquired for him shall at home be
encount'red with a shame as ample.

---

51 **pretense** intention 53 **sanctimony** holiness 57 **justified** made
certain 62 **rector** ruler (?) priest (?) 63 **intelligence** news

First Lord. The web of our life is of a mingled yarn,
   good and ill together; our virtues would be proud   *75*
   if our faults whipped them not, and our crimes
   would despair if they were not cherished by our
   virtues.

Enter a Messenger.

How now! Where's your master?

Servant. He met the Duke in the street, sir, of whom   *80*
   he hath taken a solemn leave. His lordship will next
   morning for France. The Duke hath offered him
   letters of commendations to the King.

Second Lord. They shall be no more than needful
   there, if they were more than they can commend.°   *85*

First Lord. They cannot be too sweet for the King's
   tartness.

Enter Bertram.

Here's his lordship now. How now, my lord? Is't
not after midnight?

Bertram. I have tonight dispatched sixteen businesses,   *90*
   a month's length apiece. By an abstract of success:°
   I have congied° with the Duke, done my adieu with
   his nearest, buried a wife, mourned for her, writ to
   my lady mother I am returning, entertained my
   convoy,° and between these main parcels of dis-   *95*
   patch° effected many nicer° needs; the last was the
   greatest, but that I have not ended yet.

Second Lord. If the business be of any difficulty, and
   this morning your departure hence, it requires haste
   of your lordship.

   100

84–85 **They shall . . . commend** i.e., the recommendations to the
King will not be more than needed, even if they commend Bertram
excessively (?)   91 **abstract of success** summary of my successes (?)
list, in sequence (?)   92 **congied with** taken leave of   94–95 **entertained my convoy** hired my transportation   95–96 **parcels of dispatch** things to be settled   96 **nicer** (1) more trivial (2) lascivious
(alluding to his affair with Diana)

Bertram. I mean the business is not ended, as fearing
to hear of it hereafter. But shall we have this dialogue between the Fool and the Soldier? Come,
bring forth this counterfeit module° has deceived me
105 like a double-meaning prophesier.

Second Lord. Bring him forth. [*Exeunt Soldiers.*] Has
sat i' th' stocks all night, poor gallant° knave.

Bertram. No matter, his heels have deserved it, in
usurping his spurs so long. How does he carry him-
110 self?

Second Lord. I have told your lordship already; the
stocks carry him. But to answer you as you would
be understood, he weeps like a wench that had shed
her milk. He hath confessed himself to Morgan,
115 whom he supposes to be a friar, from the time of
his remembrance to this very instant disaster of his
setting i' th' stocks. And what think you he hath
confessed?

Bertram. Nothing of me, has 'a?

120 *Second Lord.* His confession is taken, and it shall be
read to his face. If your lordship be in't, as I believe
you are, you must have the patience to hear it.

  Enter Parolles [guarded], with his Interpreter.

Bertram. A plague upon him! Muffled!° He can say
125 nothing of me.

First Lord. [*Aside to Bertram*] Hush, hush! Hoodman
comes!° [*Aloud*] Portotartarossa.

Interpreter. He calls for the tortures. What will you
say without 'em?

130 *Parolles.* I will confess what I know without constraint. If ye pinch me like a pasty I can say no
more.

104 **module** image   107 **gallant** finely dressed   124 **Muffled** blindfolded   126–27 **Hoodman comes** the blind man comes (customary
call in the game blindman's buff)

Interpreter. *Bosko chimurcho.*

Lord. *Boblibindo chicurmurco.*

Interpreter. You are a merciful general. Our General 135
bids you answer to what I shall ask you out of a
note.

Parolles. And truly, as I hope to live.

Interpreter. "First demand of him how many horse
the Duke is strong." What say you to that? 140

Parolles. Five or six thousand, but very weak and
unserviceable. The troops are all scattered and the
commanders very poor rogues, upon my reputation
and credit, and as I hope to live.

Interpreter. Shall I set down your answer so? 145

Parolles. Do. I'll take the sacrament on't, how and
which way you will.

Bertram. [*Aside*] All's one to him. What a past-saving
slave is this!

First Lord. [*Aside to Bertram*] Y'are deceived, my 150
lord; this is Monsieur Parolles, the gallant mili-
tarist—that was his own phrase—that had the
whole theoric of war in the knot of his scarf, and
the practice in the chape° of his dagger.

Second Lord. [*Aside*] I will never trust a man again 155
for keeping his sword clean, nor believe he can
have everything in him by wearing his apparel
neatly.

Interpreter. Well, that's set down.

Parolles. "Five or six thousand horse," I said—I will 160
say true—"or thereabouts" set down, for I'll speak
truth.

First Lord. [*Aside*] He's very near the truth in this.

---

154 **chape** metal plate on a scabbard covering the point

Bertram. [*Aside*] But I con° him no thanks for't, in
165 the nature he delivers it.

Parolles. "Poor rogues," I pray you say.

Interpreter. Well, that's set down.

Parolles. I humbly thank you, sir; a truth's a truth;
the rogues are marvelous poor.

170 *Interpreter.* "Demand of him of what strength they are
a-foot." What say you to that?

Parolles. By my troth, sir, if I were to live this present
hour, I will tell true. Let me see: Spurio, a hundred
and fifty; Sebastian, so many; Corambus, so many;
175 Jaques, so many; Guiltian, Cosmo, Lodowick, and
Gratii, two hundred fifty each; mine own company,
Chitopher, Vaumond, Bentii, two hundred fifty
each; so that the muster-file, rotten and sound,
upon my life, amounts not to fifteen thousand poll,°
180 half of the which dare not shake the snow from off
their cassocks° lest they shake themselves to pieces.

Bertram. [*Aside*] What shall be done to him?

First Lord. [*To Bertram*] Nothing, but let him have
thanks. [*To interpreter*] Demand of him my condi-
185 tion, and what credit I have with the Duke.

Interpreter. Well, that's set down. "You shall demand
of him whether one Captain Dumaine be i' th'
camp, a Frenchman; what his reputation is with
the Duke, what his valor, honesty, and expertness
190 in wars; or whether he thinks it were not possible
with well-weighing sums of gold to corrupt him to
a revolt." What say you to this? What do you know
of it?

Parolles. I beseech you, let me answer to the particular
195 of the inter'gatories. Demand them singly.

Interpreter. Do you know this Captain Dumaine?

164 **con** give (literally, learn)   179 **poll** head   181 **cassocks** soldiers' cloaks

Parolles. I know him; 'a was a botcher's° prentice in
Paris, from whence he was whipped for getting the
shrieve's fool° with child, a dumb innocent that
could not say him nay.   200

Bertram. [*Aside to Dumaine*] Nay, by your leave, hold
your hands, though I know his brains are forfeit to
the next tile that falls.°

Interpreter. Well, is this captain in the Duke of Florence's camp?   205

Parolles. Upon my knowledge he is, and lousy.

First Lord. [*Aside*] Nay, look not so upon me; we
shall hear of your lordship anon.

Interpreter. What is his reputation with the Duke?

Parolles. The Duke knows him for no other but a poor   210
officer of mine, and writ to me this other day to
turn him out o' th' band. I think I have his letter
in my pocket.

Interpreter. Marry, we'll search.

Parolles. In good sadness,° I do not know; either it   215
is there or it is upon a file with the Duke's other
letters in my tent.

Interpreter. Here 'tis; here's a paper; shall I read it
to you?

Parolles. I do not know if it be it or no.   220

Bertram. [*Aside*] Our interpreter does it well.

First Lord. [*Aside*] Excellently.

Interpreter. "Dian, the Count's a fool, and full of
gold."

Parolles. That is not the Duke's letter, sir; that is an

---

197 **botcher's** mender's (e.g., tailor's or cobbler's) 199 **shrieve's
fool** idiot girl placed under a sheriff's charge 203 **tile that falls**
i.e., accident 215 **sadness** seriousness

225   advertisement° to a proper maid in Florence, one
      Diana, to take heed of the allurement of one Count
      Rousillon, a foolish idle boy, but for all that very
      ruttish.° I pray you, sir, put it up again.

Interpreter. Nay, I'll read it first, by your favor.

230 *Parolles.* My meaning in't, I protest, was very honest
      in the behalf of the maid; for I knew the young
      Count to be a dangerous and lascivious boy, who
      is a whale to virginity, and devours up all the fry°
      it finds.

235 *Bertram.* [*Aside*] Damnable both-sides rogue!

Interpreter. ([*Reads a*] *letter.*) "When he swears
      oaths, bid him drop gold, and take it;
      After he scores, he never pays the score.
      Half won is match well made; match and well make
      it;°
      He ne'er pays after-debts, take it before.
240   And say a soldier, Dian, told thee this:
      Men are to mell° with, boys are not to kiss:
      For count of this, the Count's a fool, I know it,
      Who pays before, but not when he does owe it.
           Thine, as he vowed to thee in thine ear,
245   Parolles."

Bertram. [*Aside*] He shall be whipped through the
      army with this rhyme in's forehead.

Second Lord. [*Aside*] This is your devoted friend, sir,
      the manifold linguist, and the armipotent° soldier.

250 *Bertram.* [*Aside*] I could endure anything before but
      a cat, and now he's a cat to me.

Interpreter. I perceive, sir, by your General's looks,
      we shall be fain to hang you.

---

225 **advertisement** advice   228 **ruttish** lustful   233 **fry** small fish
238 **Half . . . make it** i.e., you are halfway to success if you bargain
well; so bargain well, and you will prosper (?)   241 **mell** mingle
249 **armipotent** mighty in arms (a huffing word, like "manifold")

Parolles. My life, sir, in any case! Not that I am afraid to die, but that my offenses being many I would repent out the remainder of nature. Let me live, sir, in a dungeon, i' th' stocks, or anywhere, so I may live.   255

Interpreter. We'll see what may be done, so you confess freely. Therefore once more to this Captain Dumaine: you have answered to his reputation with the Duke and to his valor: what is his honesty?   260

Parolles. He will steal, sir, an egg out of a cloister; for rapes and ravishments he parallels Nessus.° He professes not keeping of oaths, in breaking 'em he is stronger than Hercules. He will lie, sir, with such volubility that you would think truth were a fool; drunkenness is his best virtue, for he will be swine-drunk, and in his sleep he does little harm, save to his bedclothes about him; but they know his conditions° and lay him in straw. I have but little more to say, sir, of his honesty—he has everything that an honest man should not have; what an honest man should have, he has nothing.   265
                                                          270

First Lord. [*Aside*] I begin to love him for this.   275

Bertram. [*Aside*] For this description of thine honesty? A pox upon him for me, he's more and more a cat.

Interpreter. What say you to his expertness in war?

Parolles. Faith, sir, has led the drum before the English tragedians°—to belie him I will not—and more of his soldiership I know not, except in that country he had the honor to be the officer at a place there called Mile-end,° to instruct for the doubling of files.° I would do the man what honor I can, but of this I am not certain.   280
                                                          285

264 **Nessus** centaur who attempted to rape Deianira, Hercules' wife
270–71 **conditions** traits   279–80 **led . . . tragedians** i.e., been a low drummer, leading strolling actors rather than soldiers   283 **Mile-end** (because the citizen militia drilled at Mile-end, the place was a byname for military incompetence)   283–84 **doubling of files** drill maneuver in which pairs of men separate

First Lord. [*Aside*] He hath out-villained villainy so
far that the rarity redeems him.

Bertram. [*Aside*] A pox on him! He's a cat still.

Interpreter. His qualities being at this poor price, I
290   need not to ask you if gold will corrupt him to
revolt.

Parolles. Sir, for a cardecue° he will sell the fee-
simple° of his salvation, the inheritance of it, and
cut th' entail° from all remainders, and a perpetual
295   succession for it perpetually.

Interpreter. What's his brother, the other Captain
Dumaine?

Second Lord. [*Aside*] Why does he ask him of me?

Interpreter. What's he?

300   *Parolles.* E'en a crow o' th' same nest; not altogether
so great as the first in goodness, but greater a great
deal in evil. He excels his brother for a coward, yet
his brother is reputed one of the best that is. In a
retreat he outruns any lackey; marry, in coming on
305   he has the cramp.

Interpreter. If your life be saved will you undertake
to betray the Florentine?

Parolles. Ay, and the captain of his horse, Count
Rousillon.

310   *Interpreter.* I'll whisper with the General, and know
his pleasure.

Parolles. [*Aside*] I'll no more drumming. A plague of
all drums! Only to seem to deserve well, and to
beguile the supposition of that lascivious young boy,
315   the Count, have I run into this danger. Yet who
would have suspected an ambush where I was
taken?

292 **cardecue** *quart d'écu* (French coin of little value) 291–92 **fee-
simple** absolute possession 294 **entail** right of succession

Interpreter. There is no remedy, sir, but you must
die. The General says you that have so traitorously
discovered the secrets of your army and made such   *320*
pestiferous reports of men very nobly held, can
serve the world for no honest use; therefore you
must die. Come, headsman, off with his head.

Parolles. O Lord, sir, let me live, or let me see my
death!
                                                    325

Interpreter. That shall you, and take your leave of all
your friends.   [*Unmuffles Parolles.*]
So, look about you. Know you any here?

Bertram. Good morrow, noble Captain.

Second Lord. God bless you, Captain Parolles.   *330*

First Lord. God save you, noble Captain.

Second Lord. Captain, what greeting will you to my
Lord Lafew? I am for France.

First Lord. Good Captain, will you give me a copy of
the sonnet you writ to Diana in behalf of the Count   *335*
Rousillon? And I were not a very coward I'd compel it of you, but fare you well.
                              Exeunt [*Bertram and Lords*].

Interpreter. You are undone, Captain, all but your
scarf; that has a knot on't yet.

Parolles. Who cannot be crushed with a plot?   *340*

Interpreter. If you could find out a country where but
women were that had received so much shame, you
might begin an impudent nation. Fare ye well, sir.
I am for France too; we shall speak of you there.
                              Exit [*with other Soldiers*].

Parolles. Yet am I thankful. If my heart were great   *345*
'Twould burst at this. Captain I'll be no more,
But I will eat and drink and sleep as soft
As captain shall. Simply the thing I am
Shall make me live. Who knows himself a braggart,

350   Let him fear this; for it will come to pass
That every braggart shall be found an ass.
Rust, sword; cool, blushes; and Parolles live
Safest in shame! Being fooled, by fool'ry thrive!
355   There's place and means for every man alive.
I'll after them.   *Exit.*

[Scene IV. *Florence. The Widow's house.*]

Enter Helena, Widow, and Diana.

Helena. That you may well perceive I have not
wronged you,
One of the greatest in the Christian world
Shall be my surety; 'fore whose throne 'tis needful,
Ere I can perfect mine intents, to kneel.
5   Time was, I did him a desirèd office,
Dear almost as his life, which gratitude
Through flinty Tartar's bosom would peep forth,
And answer thanks. I duly am informed
His Grace is at Marseilles, to which place
10   We have convenient convoy.° You must know
I am supposèd dead. The army breaking,°
My husband hies him home, where, heaven aiding,
And by the leave of my good lord the King,
We'll be before our welcome.

Widow.   Gentle madam,
15   You never had a servant to whose trust
Your business was more welcome.

IV.iv.10 **convoy** transportation   11 **breaking** disbanding

Helena.   Nor you, mistress,
Ever a friend whose thoughts more truly labor
To recompense your love. Doubt not but heaven
Hath brought me up to be your daughter's dower,
As it hath fated her to be my motive°   20
And helper to a husband. But, O strange men,
That can such sweet use make of what they hate,
When saucy° trusting of the cozened° thoughts
Defiles the pitchy night! So lust doth play
With what it loathes for that which is away.   25
But more of this hereafter. You, Diana,
Under my poor instructions yet must suffer
Something in my behalf.

Diana.   Let death and honesty°
Go with your impositions,° I am yours
Upon your will to suffer.

Helena.   Yet, I pray you;   30
But with the word° the time will bring on summer,
When briars shall have leaves as well as thorns,
And be as sweet as sharp. We must away;
Our wagon is prepared, and time revives us.
All's well that ends well; still the fine's the crown.°   35
Whate'er the course, the end is the renown.

                                        Exeunt.

20 **motive** means (?)   23 **saucy** lascivious   23 **cozened** deceived
28 **death and honesty** an honest death   29 **impositions** tasks imposed
on me   31 **with the word** soon (?) as the proverb says (?)   35 **the
fine's the crown** the end is the crown (cf. the Latin proverb,
Finis coronat opus, "the end crowns the work")

[Scene V. *Rousillon. The Count's palace.*]

Enter Clown, Old Lady [*i.e., Countess*], *and Lafew.*

Lafew. No, no, no, your son was misled with a snipped
taffeta° fellow there, whose villainous saffron°
would have made all the unbaked and doughy
youth of a nation in his color. Your daughter-in-law
5   had been alive at this hour, and your son here at
home, more advanced by the King than by that red-
tailed humble-bee I speak of.

Countess. I would I had not known him; it was the
death of the most virtuous gentlewoman that ever
10   nature had praise for creating. If she had partaken
of my flesh and cost me the dearest groans of a
mother, I could not have owed her a more rooted
love.

Lafew. 'Twas a good lady, 'twas a good lady. We
15   may pick a thousand sallets° ere we light on such
another herb.

Clown. Indeed, sir, she was the sweet-marjoram of
the sallet, or rather, the herb of grace.°

Lafew. They are not° herbs, you knave, they are nose-
20   herbs.

Clown. I am no great Nebuchadnezzar, sir; I have
not much skill in grace.°

IV.v.1–2 **snipped taffeta** cloth slashed to show the colors beneath
2 **saffron** yellow dye (used to dye starch—for ruffs—and also dough)
15 **sallets** salads   18 **herb of grace** rue   19 **not** (pun on "knot"=
flower bed, leading to the contrasting "nose-herbs"=fragrant but not
tasty herbs)   22 **grace** (pun on "grass," following the allusion to
the King of Babylon who in Daniel 4:28–37 is said to have insanely
eaten grass)

Lafew. Whether° dost thou profess thyself, a knave or
a fool?

Clown. A fool, sir, at a woman's service, and a knave   *23*
at a man's.

Lafew. Your distinction?

Clown. I would cozen the man of his wife and do his
service.

Lafew. So you were a knave at his service indeed.   *30*

Clown. And I would give his wife my bauble,° sir,
to do her service.

Lafew. I will subscribe for thee; thou art both knave
and fool.

Clown. At your service.   *35*

Lafew. No, no, no.

Clown. Why, sir, if I cannot serve you, I can serve
as great a prince as you are.

Lafew. Who's that? A Frenchman?

Clown. Faith, sir, 'a has an English name, but his   *40*
fisnomy° is more hotter in France than there.

Lafew. What prince is that?

Clown. The Black Prince,° sir, alias the prince of
darkness, alias the devil.

Lafew. Hold thee, there's my purse. I give thee not   *45*
this to suggest thee from° thy master thou talk'st of;
serve him still.

Clown. I am a woodland fellow, sir, that always loved
a great fire, and the master I speak of ever keeps a
good fire. But sure he is the prince of the world; let   *50*
his nobility remain in's court. I am for the house

23 Whether which   31 bauble fool's stick (bawdy innuendo)   41
fisnomy physiognomy   43 Black Prince (1) son of Edward III, foe of
the French (2) devil   46 suggest thee from tempt you away from

with the narrow gate,° which I take to be too little
for pomp to enter; some that humble themselves
may, but the many will be too chill and tender, and
55 they'll be for the flow'ry way that leads to the broad
gate and the great fire.

Lafew. Go thy ways; I begin to be aweary of thee,
and I tell thee so before, because I would not fall
out with thee. Go thy ways; let my horses be well
60 looked to, without any tricks.

Clown. If I put any tricks upon 'em, sir, they shall
be jades' tricks,° which are their own right by the
law of nature.   *Exit.*

Lafew. A shrewd° knave and an unhappy.

65 *Countess.* So 'a is. My lord that's gone made himself
much sport out of him; by his authority he remains
here, which he thinks is a patent for his sauciness;
and indeed he has no pace, but runs where he will.

Lafew. I like him well, 'tis not amiss. And I was about
70 to tell you, since I heard of the good lady's death
and that my lord your son was upon his return
home, I moved the King my master to speak in the
behalf of my daughter; which, in the minority of
them both, his Majesty out of a self-gracious re-
75 membrance did first propose. His Highness hath
promised me to do it—and to stop up the displeasure he hath conceived against your son there
is no fitter matter. How does your ladyship like it?

Countess. With very much content, my lord, and I
80 wish it happily effected.

Lafew. His Highness comes post° from Marseilles, of
as able body as when he numbered thirty. 'A will
be here tomorrow, or I am deceived by him that in
such intelligence hath seldom failed.

51–52 **house with the narrow gate** heaven (with bawdy reference to
vulva?)   62 **jades' tricks** mischievous doings (like those of undesir-
able horses)   64 **shrewd** bitter   81 **post** by rapid relays of horses

Countess. It rejoices me that I hope I shall see him   85
ere I die. I have letters that my son will be here
tonight. I shall beseech your lordship to remain with
me till they meet together.

Lafew. Madam, I was thinking with what manners I
might safely be admitted.   90

Countess. You need but plead your honorable privilege.

Lafew. Lady, of that I have made a bold charter;° but
I thank my God it holds yet.

Enter Clown.

Clown. O madam, yonder's my lord your son with a   95
patch of velvet on's face; whether there be a scar
under't or no, the velvet knows, but 'tis a goodly
patch of velvet.° His left cheek is a cheek of two
pile and a half, but his right cheek is worn bare.

Lafew. A scar nobly got, or a noble scar, is a good   100
liv'ry° of honor; so belike is that.

Clown. But it is your carbonadoed° face.

Lafew. Let us go see your son, I pray you. I long to
talk with the young noble soldier.

Clown. Faith, there's a dozen of 'em with delicate   105
fine hats and most courteous feathers which bow
the head and nod at every man.   *Exeunt.*

---

93 **charter** claim   98 **patch of velvet** bandage (but it might cover an
honorable scar or dishonorable signs of syphilis)   101 **liv'ry** badge
of noble service   102 **carbonadoed** slashed (with incisions to drain
venereal ulcers)

ACT V

[Scene I. *Marseilles.*]

*Enter Helena, Widow, and Diana, with two
Attendants.*

Helena. But this exceeding posting° day and night
  Must wear your spirits low; we cannot help it.
  But since you have made the days and nights as
    one,
  To wear your gentle limbs in my affairs,
5 Be bold° you do so grow in my requital°
  As nothing can unroot you.

      Enter a Gentleman, a stranger.

                    In happy time!°
  This man may help me to his Majesty's ear,
  If he would spend his power. God save you, sir.

Gentleman. And you.

V.i.1 **exceeding posting** excessive haste 5 **bold** assured 5 **requital** debt 6 **In happy time** just at the right moment

Helena. Sir, I have seen you in the court of France.   10

Gentleman. I have been sometimes there.

Helena. I do presume, sir, that you are not fall'n
From the report that goes upon your goodness,
And therefore, goaded with most sharp occasions
Which lay nice manners by, I put you to   15
The use of your own virtues, for the which
I shall continue thankful.

Gentleman.   What's your will?

Helena. That it will please you
To give this poor petition to the King,
And aid me with that store of power you have   20
To come into his presence.

Gentleman. The King's not here.

Helena.   Not here, sir?

Gentleman.   Not indeed.
He hence removed last night, and with more haste
Than is his use.

Widow.   Lord, how we lose our pains!

Helena. All's well that ends well yet,   25
Though time seem so adverse and means unfit.
I do beseech you, whither is he gone?

Gentleman. Marry, as I take it, to Rousillon,
Whither I am going.

Helena.   I do beseech you, sir,
Since you are like to see the King before me,
Commend the paper to his gracious hand,   30
Which I presume shall render you no blame
But rather make you thank your pains for it.
I will come after you with what good speed
Our means will make us means.

Gentleman.   This I'll do for you.   35

Helena. And you shall find yourself to be well
   thanked,
Whate'er falls° more. We must to horse again.
Go, go, provide.   [*Exeunt.*]

[Scene II. *Rousillon. The Count's palace.*]

Enter Clown and Parolles.

Parolles. Good Master Lavatch,° give my Lord
   Lafew this letter. I have ere now, sir, been better
   known to you, when I have held familiarity with
   fresher clothes; but I am now, sir, muddied in for-
5   tune's mood,° and smell somewhat strong of her
   strong displeasure.

Clown. Truly, fortune's displeasure is but sluttish if
   it smell so strongly as thou speak'st of. I will hence-
   forth eat no fish of fortune's butt'ring. Prithee,
10   allow the wind.°

Parolles. Nay, you need not to stop your nose, sir;
   I spake but by a metaphor.

Clown. Indeed, sir, if your metaphor stink, I will stop
   my nose, or against any man's metaphor. Prithee,
15   get thee further.

Parolles. Pray you, sir, deliver me this paper.

Clown. Foh! Prithee, stand away. A paper from for-

---

37 **falls** befalls   V.ii.1 **Lavatch** (apparently from French *la vache*=
the cow, or *lavage*=slop)   5 **mood** displeasure (with pun on mud)
10 **allow the wind** let me have the windward side

tune's close-stool,° to give to a nobleman! Look,
here he comes himself.

Enter Lafew.

Here is a pur° of fortune's, sir, or of fortune's   20
cat, but not a musk-cat,° that has fall'n into the
unclean fishpond of her displeasure, and, as he
says, is muddied withal. Pray you, sir, use the carp
as you may, for he looks like a poor, decayed, ingenious,° foolish, rascally knave. I do pity his dis-   25
tress in my similes of comfort, and leave him to
your lordship.

[*Exit.*]

Parolles. My lord, I am a man whom fortune hath
cruelly scratched.

Lafew. And what would you have me to do? 'Tis too   30
late to pare her nails now. Wherein have you
played the knave with fortune that she should
scratch you, who of herself is a good lady and
would not have knaves thrive long under? There's
a cardecue° for you. Let the justices make you and   35
fortune friends;° I am for other business.

Parolles. I beseech your honor to hear me one single
word.

Lafew. You beg a single penny more. Come, you shall
ha't; save your word.   40

Parolles. My name, my good lord, is Parolles.

Lafew. You beg more than "word" then. Cox my
passion!° Give me your hand. How does your
drum?

---

18 **close-stool** toilet   20 **pur** (1) dung (2) cat's sound (3) knave in
a card game (Lafew picks up this last meaning when he speaks)
21 **musk-cat** musk deer (which yields perfume)   24–25 **ingenious**
stupid (as though written "un-genius")   35 **cardecue** French coin
35–36 **Let . . . friends** i.e., appeal to the justices for alms   42–43
Cox my passion (mild oath, from "God's my passion," i.e., by God's
suffering)

45 *Parolles.* O my good lord, you were the first that
    found me.°

    Lafew. Was I, in sooth? And I was the first that lost
    thee.

    Parolles. It lies in you, my lord, to bring me in some
50 grace, for you did bring me out.

    Lafew. Out upon thee, knave! Dost thou put upon
    me at once both the office of God and the devil?
    One brings thee in grace and the other brings thee
    out. [*Trumpets sound.*] The King's coming; I know
55 by his trumpets. Sirrah, inquire further after me.
    I had talk of you last night; though you are a fool
    and a knave you shall eat. Go to, follow.

    Parolles. I praise God for you.   [*Exeunt.*]

[Scene III. *Rousillon. The Count's palace.*]

    Flourish. Enter King, Old Lady [*i.e., Countess*],
    Lafew, the two French Lords, with Attendants.

    King. We lost a jewel of her, and our esteem°
       Was made much poorer by it; but your son,
       As mad in folly, lacked the sense to know
       Her estimation home.°

    Countess.   'Tis past, my liege,

46 found me found me out   V.iii.1 esteem value, i.e., reputation
4 home fully

And I beseech your Majesty to make it   5
Natural rebellion done i' th' blade° of youth,
When oil and fire, too strong for reason's force,
O'erbears it and burns on.

King.   My honored lady,
I have forgiven and forgotten all,
Though my revenges were high bent upon him   10
And watched the time to shoot.

Lafew.   This I must say—
But first I beg my pardon—the young lord
Did to his Majesty, his mother, and his lady
Offense of mighty note, but to himself
The greatest wrong of all. He lost a wife   15
Whose beauty did astonish the survey
Of richest eyes; whose words all ears took captive;
Whose dear perfection hearts that scorned to serve
Humbly called mistress.

King.   Praising what is lost
Makes the remembrance dear. Well, call him
    hither;
                                                    20
We are reconciled, and the first view shall kill
All repetition.° Let him not ask our pardon;
The nature of his great offense is dead,
And deeper than oblivion we do bury
Th' incensing relics° of it. Let him approach,   25
A stranger, no offender; and inform him
So 'tis our will he should.

Gentleman.   I shall, my liege.   [*Exit.*]

King. What says he to your daughter? Have you
    spoke?

Lafew. All that he is hath reference° to your High-
    ness.

___

6 **blade** green shoot (editors distressed by the mixed metaphor produced by "fire" emend to "blaze")   22 **repetition** i.e., mention of
what is past   25 **incensing relics** reminders that (would) anger   29
hath reference is submitted

King. Then shall we have a match. I have letters sent
30   me,
    That sets him high in fame.

Enter Bertram.

Lafew.   He looks well on't.

King. I am not a day of season,
    For thou mayst see a sunshine and a hail
    In me at once. But to the brightest beams
35   Distracted clouds give way; so stand thou forth;
    The time is fair again.

Bertram.   My high-repented blames,°
    Dear sovereign pardon to me.

King.   All is whole.
    Not one word more of the consumèd time.
    Let's take the instant by the forward top;°
40   For we are old, and on our quick'st decrees
    Th' inaudible and noiseless foot of Time
    Steals ere we can effect them. You remember
    The daughter of this lord?

Bertram. Admiringly, my liege. At first
45   I stuck my choice upon her, ere my heart
    Durst make too bold a herald of my tongue;
    Where, the impression of mine eye infixing,
    Contempt his scornful perspective° did lend me,
    Which warped the line of every other favor,°
50   Scorned a fair color or expressed it stol'n,
    Extended or contracted all proportions
    To a most hideous object. Thence it came
    That she whom all men praised and whom myself,
    Since I have lost, have loved, was in mine eye
    The dust that did offend it.

55 *King.*   Well excused.
    That thou didst love her, strikes some scores away

---

36 **blames** blameworthy deeds   39 **take . . . top** seize Time by the
forelock   48 **perspective** optical instrument that distorts (accented
on first syllable)   49 **favor** face

From the great compt;° but love that comes too
  late,
Like a remorseful° pardon slowly carried,
To the great sender turns a sour offense,
Crying "That's good that's gone." Our rash faults   60
Make trivial price of serious things we have,
Not knowing them, until we know their grave.
Oft our displeasures, to ourselves unjust,
Destroy our friends and after weep their dust;
Our own love waking cries to see what's done,   65
While shameful hate sleeps out the afternoon.
Be this sweet Helen's knell, and now forget her.
Send forth your amorous token for fair Maudlin.
The main consents are had, and here we'll stay
To see our widower's second marriage-day,   70
Which better than the first, O dear heaven, bless!
Or, ere they meet, in me, O nature, cesse!°

Lafew. Come on, my son, in whom my house's name
Must be digested;° give a favor° from you
To sparkle in the spirits of my daughter,   75
That she may quickly come. [*Bertram gives a ring.*]
  By my old beard,
And ev'ry hair that's on't, Helen that's dead
Was a sweet creature; such a ring as this,
The last that e'er I took her leave at court,
I saw upon her finger.

Bertram.   Hers it was not.   80

King. Now pray you let me see it; for mine eye,
While I was speaking, oft was fastened to't.
This ring was mine, and when I gave it Helen
I bade her, if her fortunes ever stood
Necessitied to help, that by this token   85
I would relieve her. Had you that craft to reave°
  her
Of what should stead° her most?

---

57 **compt** account   58 **remorseful** compassionate   72 **cesse** cease
74 **digested** swallowed up (?) assimilated (?)   74 **favor** token
86 **reave** deprive   87 **stead** help

Bertram.   My gracious sovereign,
     Howe'er it pleases you to take it so,
     The ring was never hers.

Countess.   Son, on my life,
90   I have seen her wear it, and she reckoned it
     At her life's rate.

Lafew.   I am sure I saw her wear it.

Bertram. You are deceived, my lord; she never saw it.
     In Florence was it from a casement thrown me,
     Wrapped in a paper which contained the name
95   Of her that threw it. Noble she was, and thought
     I stood ingaged;° but when I had subscribed
     To mine own fortune° and informed her fully
     I could not answer in that course of honor
     As she had made the overture, she ceased
100 In heavy satisfaction° and would never
     Receive the ring again.

King.   Plutus° himself,
     That knows the tinct and multiplying med'cine,°
     Hath not in nature's mystery more science°
     Than I have in this ring. 'Twas mine, 'twas Helen's,
105 Whoever gave it you; then if you know
     That you are well acquainted with yourself,
     Confess 'twas hers, and by what rough enforcement
     You got it from her. She called the saints to surety
     That she would never put it from her finger
110 Unless she gave it to yourself in bed,
     Where you have never come, or sent it us
     Upon her great disaster.

Bertram.   She never saw it.

King. Thou speak'st it falsely, as I love mine honor,
     And mak'st conjectural fears to come into me

---

96 **ingaged** not pledged (to another woman)   96–97 **subscribed/To
mine own fortune** admitted my condition, i.e., that I was married
100 **heavy satisfaction** sorrowful acceptance   101 **Plutus** god of
wealth   102 **tinct and multiplying med'cine** elixir that transmutes
base metals to gold and multiplies gold   103 **science** knowledge

Which I would fain shut out. If it should prove   115
That thou art so inhuman—'twill not prove so,
And yet I know not—thou didst hate her deadly,
And she is dead, which nothing but to close
Her eyes myself could win me to believe,
More than to see this ring. Take him away.   120
My fore-past proofs, howe'er the matter fall,
Shall tax my fears of little vanity,
Having vainly feared too little.° Away with him,
We'll sift this matter further.

Bertram.   If you shall prove
This ring was ever hers, you shall as easy   125
Prove that I husbanded her bed in Florence,
Where yet she never was.   [*Exit guarded.*]

King. I am wrapped in dismal thinkings.

          Enter a Gentleman, [the stranger].

Gentleman.   Gracious sovereign,
Whether I have been to blame or no, I know not:
Here's a petition from a Florentine   130
Who hath for four or five removes° come short
To tender it herself. I undertook it,
Vanquished thereto by the fair grace and speech
Of the poor suppliant, who, by this, I know
Is here attending; her business looks in her   135
With an importing° visage, and she told me,
In a sweet verbal brief, it did concern
Your Highness with herself.

[*King reads*] *a letter.* "Upon his many protestations
to marry me when his wife was dead, I blush to   140
say it, he won me. Now is the Count Rousillon a
widower, his vows are forfeited to me, and my
honor's paid to him. He stole from Florence, taking
no leave, and I follow him to his country for justice.

121–23 **My fore-past . . . too little** the evidence already established,
however the affair turns out, will rebuke ("tax") my lightweight
("of little vanity") fears; I have unreasonably feared too little
131 **removes** stopping places (changes of residence) on the King's
journey   136 **importing** significant

145 Grant it me, O King! In you it best lies; otherwise a
seducer flourishes and a poor maid is undone.
                              Diana Capilet."

Lafew. I will buy me a son-in-law in a fair, and toll
for° this. I'll none of him.

150 *King.* The heavens have thought well on thee, Lafew,
To bring forth this discov'ry. Seek these suitors.
                              [*Exeunt Attendants.*]
Go, speedily and bring again the Count.
I am afeard the life of Helen, lady,
Was foully snatched.

Countess.   Now, justice on the doers!

                    Enter Bertram, [guarded].

155 *King.* I wonder, sir, since wives are monsters to you,
And that you fly them as you swear them lordship,
Yet you desire to marry.

                    Enter Widow [and] Diana.

                              What woman's that?

Diana. I am, my lord, a wretched Florentine,
Derivèd from the ancient Capilet.
160 My suit, as I do understand, you know,
And therefore know how far I may be pitied.

Widow. I am her mother, sir, whose age and honor
Both suffer under this complaint we bring,
And both shall cease, without your remedy.°

King. Come hither, Count—do you know these
165 women?

Bertram. My lord, I neither can nor will deny
But that I know them. Do they charge me further?

Diana. Why do you look so strange upon your wife?

148–49 **toll for** put up for sale   164 **both . . . remedy** both my life
("age") and honor will die unless you give us relief (by having
Bertram marry Diana)

Bertram. She's none of mine, my lord.

Diana.   If you shall marry,
  You give away this hand, and that is mine;   *170*
  You give away heaven's vows, and those are mine;
  You give away myself, which is known mine;
  For I by vow am so embodied yours
  That she which marries you must marry me,
  Either both or none.   *175*

Lafew. Your reputation comes too short for my
  daughter; you are no husband for her.

Bertram. My lord, this is a fond° and desp'rate crea-
  ture,
  Whom sometime I have laughed with. Let your
  Highness
  Lay a more noble thought upon mine honor,   *180*
  Than for to think that I would sink it here.

King. Sir, for my thoughts, you have them ill to
  friend
  Till your deeds gain them; fairer prove your honor
  Than in my thought it lies.

Diana.   Good my lord,
  Ask him upon his oath if he does think   *185*
  He had not my virginity.

King. What say'st thou to her?

Bertram.   She's impudent, my lord,
  And was a common gamester° to the camp.

Diana. He does me wrong, my lord; if I were so,
  He might have bought me at a common price.
  Do not believe him. O, behold this ring,   *190*
  Whose high respect and rich validity
  Did lack a parallel; yet for all that
  He gave it to a commoner o' th' camp,
  If I be one.

Countess.   He blushes, and 'tis hit!   *195*

178 **fond** foolish   188 **gamester** prostitute

Of six preceding ancestors, that gem,
Conferred by testament to th' sequent issue,°
Hath it been owed° and worn. This is his wife,
That ring's a thousand proofs.

King.   Methought you said
200 You saw one here in court could witness it.

Diana. I did, my lord, but loath am to produce
So bad an instrument. His name's Parolles.

Lafew. I saw the man today, if man he be.

King. Find him and bring him hither.
                            [*Exit an Attendant.*]

Bertram.   What of him?
205 He's quoted for° a most perfidious slave,
With all the spots o' th' world taxed and deboshed,°
Whose nature sickens but to speak a truth.
Am I or that or this for what he'll utter,
That will speak anything?

King.   She hath that ring of yours.

210 *Bertram.* I think she has. Certain it is I liked her,
And boarded her i' th' wanton way of youth.
She knew her distance, and did angle for me,
Madding my eagerness with her restraint,
As all impediments in fancy's° course
215 Are motives of more fancy; and in fine
Her inf'nite cunning with her modern° grace
Subdued me to her rate. She got the ring,
And I had that which any inferior might
At market-price have bought.

Diana.   I must be patient:
220 You that have turned off a first so noble wife,
May justly diet° me. I pray you yet—
Since you lack virtue I will lose a husband—

---

197 **sequent issue** next heir   198 **owed** owned   205 **quoted for**
known as   206 **taxed and deboshed** censured as debauched   214
fancy's love's   216 **modern** commonplace   221 **diet** restrain yourself from

Send for your ring, I will return it home,
And give me mine again.

Bertram.   I have it not.

King. What ring was yours, I pray you?

Diana.   Sir, much like   *225*
The same upon your finger.

King. Know you this ring? This ring was his of late.

Diana. And this was it I gave him, being abed.

King. The story then goes false you threw it him
Out of a casement?

Diana.   I have spoke the truth.   *230*

Enter Parolles.

Bertram. My lord, I do confess, the ring was hers.

King. You boggle shrewdly;° every feather starts you.
Is this the man you speak of?

Diana.   Ay, my lord.

King. Tell me, sirrah, but tell me true, I charge you,
Not fearing the displeasure of your master,   *235*
Which on your just proceeding I'll keep off—
By him and by this woman here what know you?

Parolles. So please your Majesty, my master hath been
an honorable gentleman. Tricks he hath had in him,
which gentlemen have.   *240*

King. Come, come, to th' purpose: did he love this
woman?

Parolles. Faith, sir, he did love her; but how?

King. How, I pray you?

Parolles. He did love her, sir, as a gentleman loves a   *245*
woman.°

---

232 **boggle shrewdly** startle excessively   246 **woman** (in contrast to
a highborn lady)

King. How is that?

Parolles. He loved her, sir, and loved her not.°

King. As thou art a knave and no knave. What an
250   equivocal companion° is this!

Parolles. I am a poor man, and at your Majesty's
  command.

Lafew. He's a good drum, my lord, but a naughty°
  orator.

253 *Diana.* Do you know he promised me marriage?

Parolles. Faith, I know more than I'll speak.

King. But wilt thou not speak all thou know'st?

Parolles. Yes, so please your Majesty. I did go between them as I said; but more than that, he loved
260   her, for indeed he was mad for her and talked of
  Satan and of Limbo and of Furies and I know not
  what; yet I was in that credit with them at that time
  that I knew of their going to bed and of other mo-
  tions, as promising her marriage, and things which
265   would derive me ill will to speak of; therefore I will
  not speak what I know.

King. Thou hast spoken all already, unless thou canst
  say they are married. But thou art too fine° in thy
  evidence; therefore stand aside.
  This ring, you say, was yours?

270 *Diana.*   Ay, my good lord.

King. Where did you buy it? Or who gave it you?

Diana. It was not given me, nor I did not buy it.

King. Who lent it you?

Diana.   It was not lent me neither.

---

248 **not** (perhaps punning on "knot" = maidenhead)   250 **equivocal
companion** equivocating fellow ("companion" is contemptuous)
253 **naughty** (1) worthless, worth naught (2) wicked   268 **fine** subtle

King. Where did you find it then?

Diana.   I found it not.

King. If it were yours by none of all these ways,   275
  How could you give it him?

Diana.   I never gave it him.

Lafew. This woman's an easy glove, my lord; she goes
  off and on at pleasure.

King. This ring was mine; I gave it his first wife.

Diana. It might be yours or hers for aught I know.   280

King. Take her away; I do not like her now.
  To prison with her. And away with him.
  Unless thou tell'st me where thou hadst this ring
  Thou diest within this hour.

Diana.   I'll never tell you.

King. Take her away.

Diana.   I'll put in bail, my liege.   285

King. I think thee now some common customer.°

Diana. By Jove, if ever I knew man, 'twas you.

King. Wherefore hast thou accused him all this while?

Diana. Because he's guilty and he is not guilty:
  He knows I am no maid, and he'll swear to't: 290
  I'll swear I am a maid and he knows not.
  Great King, I am no strumpet; by my life
  I am either maid or else this old man's wife.

King. She does abuse our ears. To prison with her!

Diana. Good mother, fetch my bail.   [*Exit Widow.*]
    Stay, royal sir,   295
  The jeweler that owes the ring is sent for
  And he shall surety me. But for this lord
  Who hath abused me as he knows himself,

286 **customer** prostitute

Though yet he never harmed me, here I quit° him.
300 He knows himself my bed he hath defiled,
And at that time he got his wife with child.
Dead though she be, she feels her young one kick.
So there's my riddle: one that's dead is quick.°
And now behold the meaning.

Enter Helena and Widow.

King.   Is there no exorcist°
305 Beguiles the truer office of mine eyes?
Is't real that I see?

Helena.   No, my good lord,
'Tis but the shadow of a wife you see,
The name and not the thing.

Bertram.   Both, both. O, pardon!

Helena. O, my good lord, when I was like° this maid,
310 I found you wondrous kind. There is your ring,
And, look you, here's your letter. This it says:
"When from my finger you can get this ring,
And is by me with child," &c. This is done.
Will you be mine, now you are doubly won?

Bertram. If she, my liege, can make me know this
315   clearly,
I'll love her dearly, ever, ever dearly.

Helena. If it appear not plain and prove untrue,
Deadly divorce step between me and you!
O, my dear mother, do I see you living?

320 *Lafew.* Mine eyes smell onions, I shall weep anon.
[*To Parolles*] Good Tom Drum, lend me a handker-
cher. So, I thank thee. Wait on me home, I'll make
sport with thee. Let thy curtsies alone, they are
scurvy ones.

325 *King.* Let us from point to point this story know,
To make the even truth in pleasure flow.

299 **quit** acquit   303 **quick** (1) alive (2) pregnant   304 **exorcist**
summoner of spirits   309 **like** i.e., substitute for

[*To Diana*] If thou be'st yet a fresh uncroppèd
    flower,
Choose thou thy husband, and I'll pay thy dower,
For I can guess that by thy honest aid
Thou kept'st a wife herself, thyself a maid.   *330*
Of that and all the progress more and less
Resolvedly° more leisure shall express.
All yet seems well, and if it end so meet,
The bitter past, more welcome is the sweet.
                                        Flourish.

[*Epilogue*]

The King's a beggar° now the play is done.
All is well ended if this suit be won,
That you express content; which we will pay
With strife° to please you, day exceeding day.
Ours be your patience then, and yours our parts,°   *5*
Your gentle hands lend us, and take our hearts.
                                Exeunt omnes.

FINIS

332 **Resolvedly** so that doubt is removed   Epilogue 1 **beggar** i.e.,
for applause   4 **strife** striving   5 **Ours . . . parts** i.e., we will
silently listen, as you have done, and you are now the performers

Textual Note

A bookseller's reference in 1603 to "love's labor won" suggests that there was by that date a published version of a play so entitled. No copies survive. Some scholars identify this title with *All's Well,* but whatever the validity of the identification, the only authoritative text for *All's Well* is that of the First Folio (1623). Exactly what sort of text for this play the Folio's editors worked from is not certain, but probably it was either Shakespeare's finished manuscript or a scribe's copy of the manuscript. The play seems complete; it is not, for example, notably short, like *Timon of Athens,* and although it has some loose ends, they do not bulk large, as they do in *Timon,* which must be incomplete. There are, of course, puzzling words and lines, possibly as a result of a scribe's failure to transcribe accurately, and there are signs that a little tidying up remained to be done. For example, there is some inconsistency in the assignment of speeches to the two French lords, and some of their speeches are puzzlingly designated "G" and "E"—possibly the initials of actors for whom the speeches were written. And in a stage direction at III.v there is given the name "Violenta," yet no such character speaks or is addressed. Possibly Violenta was Shakespeare's first thought of a name for the widow's daughter, who is later called Diana, or possibly Violenta is a character that Shakespeare at first believed he would use in the scene but (as he worked further into the scene) decided was of no use. In a way, these minor confusions are reassuring; they suggest we have the play as Shakespeare wrote it, rather than a neat stage version that perhaps omits some of his material.

The Signet text modernizes spelling and punctuation, expands abbreviations, straightens out some confusion in the assignment of lines to the First and Second Lords, regularizes speech prefixes (e.g., the Folio's "Mother," "Mo.," "Coun[tess]," "La[dy]," etc., all are given as "Countess"), and regularly gives in the stage directions "Bertram" (for the Folio's "Count," or "Count Rosse," etc.) and "Helena" (because the Folio's first stage direction and first reference to her in dialogue call her so, though the Folio later calls her "Helen"). The act divisions are translated from Latin into English. The Folio does not divide the play into scenes, giving only "Actus Primus. Scoena Prima," but the conventional and convenient scene divisions of the Globe text have been given here. These additions, and others (locales and necessary stage directions not found in the Folio) have been placed in square brackets. The position of an authentic stage direction has occasionally been slightly altered when necessary, and some passages that are printed as prose in the Folio are printed as verse here. Other substantial departures from the Folio are listed below, the present reading given first, in italic type, followed by the original reading, in roman.

I.i.134 *got* goe   155 *ten* two   165 *wear* were

I.iii.19 *I* w   115 *Diana no queen* Queene   173 *loneliness* louelinesse   179 *t'one to th'other* 'ton tooth to th'other   204 *inteemable* intemible   237 *Haply* Happily

II.i.43 *with his cicatrice, an emblem* his sicatrice, with an Embleme   64 *fee* see   146 *sits* shifts   157 *impostor* Impostrue   194 *heaven* helpe

II.ii.63 *An* And

II.iii.95 *her* heere   126 *when* whence   131 *it is* is is   295 *detested* detected

II.v.27 *End* And   29 *one* on   52 *think not* thinke

III.i.23 *the* th the

III.ii.9 *sold* hold   19 *E'en* In   115 *still-piecing* still-peering

III.v.s.d. *her daughter Diana* her daughter, Violenta   34 *le* la
66 *warrant* write

III.vi.36 *his* this   37 *ore* ours

III.vii.19 *Resolved* Resolue

IV.i.91 *art* are

IV.iii.86–89 *They ... midnight* [Folio gives to Bertram]   126 *Hush,
hush* [Folio gives to Bertram]   148 *All's . . . him* [Folio gives to
Parolles]   208 *lordship* Lord

IV.iv.9 *Marseilles* Marcella   16 *you* your

IV.v.40 *name* maine   81 *Marseilles* Marcellus

V.i.6.s.d. *Gentleman, a stranger* gentle Astringer

V.ii.26 *similes* smiles

V.iii.122 *tax* taze   155 *since* sir   157s.d. *Widow* [*and*] *Diana* Wid-
dow, Diana, and Parolles   216 *inf'nite cunning* insuite comming

Epilogue 4 *strife* strift

The Source of
All's Well That Ends Well

All's Well is derived from the ninth story of the third day of Boccaccio's *Decameron* (written 1348–58), presumably in William Painter's translation in *The Palace of Pleasure*. (Nothing is gained by assuming that Shakespeare used a French translation of Boccaccio.) As even a casual reading of story and play will show, Shakespeare made substantial additions, and a few deletions, altering a well-told but scarcely brilliant or weighty little tale into a play of considerable subtlety and density.

Painter's translation appeared in the first edition (1566) of *The Palace,* but the version given below is the revision in the third edition (1575), which, because later, Shakespeare is more likely to have had at hand. In any case, the alterations are slight and there are no differences important to the student of Shakespeare. Spelling and punctuation have been modernized, and two errors in pronouns have been corrected.

WILLIAM PAINTER

from *The Palace of Pleasure*

THE THIRTY-EIGHTH NOVEL

Giletta, a physician's daughter of Narbon, healed the French King of a fistula, for reward whereof she demanded Beltramo, Count of Rossiglione, to husband. The Count being married against his will, for despite fled to Florence and loved another. Giletta, his wife, by policy found means to lie with her husband, in place of his lover, and was begotten with child of two sons; which known to her husband, he received her again, and afterwards he lived in great honor and felicity.

In France there was a gentleman called Isnardo, the Count of Rossiglione, who, because he was sickly and diseased, kept always in his house a physician, named Master Gerardo of Narbona. This Count had only one son called Beltramo, a very young child, amiable and fair; with whom there was nourished and brought up many other children of his age, amongs whom one of the daughters of the said physician, named Giletta, who fervently fell in love with Beltramo, more than was meet for a maiden of her age. This Beltramo, when his father was dead, and left under the royal custody of the King, was sent to Paris, for whose departure the maiden was very pensive. A little while after, her father being likewise dead, she was desirous to go to Paris, only to see the young Count, if for that purpose she could get any good occasion. But being diligently looked unto by her kinsfolk (because she was rich and fatherless) she could see no convenient way for her intended journey; and being now marriageable, the love she bare to the Count was never out of her remembrance, and refused many husbands with whom her kinsfolk would have matched her, without making them privy to the cause of her refusal. Now it chanced that she burned more in love with Beltramo than ever she did before, because she heard tell that he was grown to the state of a goodly young gentleman. She heard by report that the French King had a swelling upon his breast which by reason of ill cure was grown to be a fistula, which did put him to marvelous pain and grief, and that there was no physician to be found (although many were proved) that could heal it, but rather did impair the grief and made it worse and worse. Wherefore the King, like one in despair, would take no more counsel or help. Whereof the young maiden was wonderful glad, thinking to have by this means not only a lawful occasion to go to Paris, but if the discase were such (as she supposed) easily to bring to pass that she might have the Count Beltramo to her husband. Whereupon with such knowledge as she had learned at her father's hands beforetime, she made a powder of certain herbs, which she thought meet for that disease, and rode to Paris. And the first thing she went about when she came thither was to see the Count Beltramo. And then she repaired to the King, praying his Grace to vouchsafe to show her his grief. The King, perceiving her to be a fair young maiden and a comely, would not hide it, but opened the same unto her. So soon as she saw it she put him in comfort that she was able to heal him, saying, "Sir, if it may please your Grace, I trust in God, without any great pain unto your Highness, within eight days to make you whole of this disease." The King, hearing her say so, began to mock her, saying, "How is it possible for thee, being a young woman, to do that which the best renowned physicians in the world cannot?" He thanked her for her goodwill and made her a direct answer, that he was determined no more to follow the counsel of any physician. Whereunto the maiden answered, "Sir, you despise my knowledge because I am young and a woman, but I assure you that I do not minister physic by profession but by the aid and help of God; and with the cunning of Master Gerardo of Narbona, who was my father and a physician of great fame so long as he lived." The King, hearing these words, said to himself, "This woman, aperadventure, is sent unto me of God, and therefore why should I disdain to prove her cunning, for so much as she promiseth to heal me within a little space without any offense or grief unto me?" And being determined to prove her, he said, "Damsel, if thou dost not heal me, but make me to break my determination, what wilt thou shall follow thereof?" "Sir," said the maiden, "let me be kept in what guard and keeping you list, and if I do not heal you within these eight days let me be burned; but if I do heal your Grace, what recompense shall I have then?" To whom the King answered, "Because thou art a maiden and unmarried, if thou heal me according to thy promise, I will bestow thee upon some gentleman that shall be of right good worship and estimation." To whom she answered, "Sir, I am very well content that you bestow me in marriage; but I beseech your Grace let me have such a husband as I myself shall demand, without presumption to any of your children or other of your blood." Which request the King incontinently granted. The young maiden began to minister her physic, and in short space before her appointed time she had throughly cured the King. And when the King perceived himself whole, said unto her, "Thou hast well deserved a husband, Giletta, even such a one as thyself shalt choose." "I have then, my lord," quoth she, "deserved the County Beltramo of Rossiglione, whom I have loved from my youth." The King was very loath to grant him unto her, but for that he had made a promise, which he was loath to break, he caused him to be called forth, and said unto him: "Sir County, knowing full well that you are a gentleman of great honor, our pleasure is that you return home to your own house, to order your estate according to your degree; and that you take with you a damsel which I have appointed to be your wife." To whom the County gave his humble thanks and demanded what she was. "It is she," quoth the King, "that with her medicines hath healed me." The Count knew her well, and had already seen her, although she was fair, yet knowing her not to be of a stock convenable to his nobility, scornfully said unto the King, "Will you then, sir, give me a physician to wife? It is not the pleasure of God that ever I should in that wise bestow myself." To whom the King said, "Wilt thou then that we should break our faith, which we to recover health, have given to the damsel, who for a reward asked thee to husband?" "Sir," quoth Beltramo, "you may take from me all that I have and give my person to whom you please because I am your subject; but I assure you I shall never be contented with that marriage." "Well, you shall have her," said the King, "for the maiden is fair and wise and loveth you most entirely, thinking verily you shall lead a more joyful life with her than with a lady of a greater house." The County therewithal held his peace, and the King made great preparation for the marriage. And when the appointed day was come, the Count in the presence of the King (although it were against his will) married the maiden, who loved him better than her own self. Which done, the Count, determining before what he would do, prayed license to return to his country to consummate the marriage. And when he was on horseback he went not thither, but took his journey into Tuscane, where, understanding that the Florentines and Senoys were at wars, he determined to take the Florentines' part, and was willingly received and honorably entertained and was made captain of a certain number of men, continuing in their service a long time. The new-married gentlewoman, scarce contented with his unkindness, hoping by her well-doing to cause him to return into his country, went to Rossiglione, where she was received of all his subjects for their lady. And perceiving that through the Count's absence all things were spoiled and out of order, she, like a sage lady, with great diligence and care disposed his things in order again, whereof the subjects rejoiced very much, bearing to her their hearty love and affection, greatly blaming the Count because he could not content himself with her. This notable gentlewoman, having restored all the country again to their ancient liberties, sent word to the Count, her husband, by two knights to signify unto him that if it were for her sake that he had abandoned his country, upon return of answer she to do him pleasure would depart from thence. To whom he churlishly replied, "Let her do what she list. For I do purpose to dwell with her when she shall have this ring (meaning a ring which he wore) upon her finger, and a son in her arms begotten by me." He greatly loved that ring and kept it very carefully and never took it from his finger for a certain virtue that he knew it had. The knights, hearing the hard condition of two things impossible, and seeing that by them he could not be removed from his determination, returned again to the lady, telling her his answer, who very sorrowful, after she had a good while bethought her, purposed to find means to attain the two things, that thereby she might recover her husband. And having advised herself what to do, she assembled the noblest and chiefest of her country, declaring unto them in lamentable wise what she had already done to win the love of the Count, showing them also what followed thereof. And in the end said unto them that she was loath the Count for her sake should dwell in perpetual exile; therefore she determined to spend the rest of her time in pilgrimages and devotion for preservation of her soul, praying them to take the charge and government of the country and that they would let the Count understand that she had forsaken his house and was removed far from thence, with purpose never to return to Rossiglione again. Many tears were shed by the people as she was speaking those words, and divers supplications were made unto her to alter her opinion, but all in vain. Wherefore commending them all unto God she took her way, with her maid and one of her kinsmen, in the habit of a pilgrim, well furnished with silver and precious jewels, telling no man whither she went, and never rested till she came to Florence, where, arriving by fortune at a poor widow's house, she contented herself with the state of a poor pilgrim, desirous to hear news of her lord whom by fortune she saw the next day passing by the house (where she lay) on horseback with his company. And although she knew him well enough, yet she demanded of the good wife of the house what he was, who answered that he was a strange gentleman called the Count Beltramo of Rossiglione, a courteous knight and well beloved in the city, and that he was marvelously in love with a neighbor of hers that was a gentlewoman, very poor and of small substance, nevertheless of right honest life and good report, and by reason of her poverty was yet unmarried and dwelt with her mother, that was a wise and honest lady. The Countess, well noting these words, and by little and little debating every particular point thereof, comprehending the effect of those news, concluded what to do, and when she had well understanded which was the house and the name of the lady and of her daughter that was beloved of the Count, upon a day repaired to the house secretly, in the habit of a pilgrim, where finding the mother and daughter in poor estate amongs their family, after she had saluted them told the mother that she had to say unto her. The gentlewoman rising up courteously entertained her, and being entered alone in a chamber they sat down, and the Countess began to speak unto her in this wise. "Madam, methink that ye be one upon whom fortune doth frown, so well as upon me; but if you please, you may both comfort me and yourself." The lady answered that there was nothing in the world whereof she was more desirous than of honest comfort. The Countess proceeding in her talk said unto her, "I have need now of your fidelity and trust, whereupon if I do stay and you deceive me you shall both undo me and yourself." "Tell me then what it is, hardly," said the gentlewoman, "for you shall never be deceived of me." Then the Countess began to recite her her whole estate of love, telling her what she was and what had chanced to that present day, in such perfit order as the gentlewoman believing her, because she had partly heard report before, began to have compassion upon her, and after that the Countess had rehearsed the whole circumstance, she continued her purpose, saying, "Now you have heard amongs other my troubles what two things they be which behooveth me to have if I do recover my husband, which I know none can help me to obtain but only you, if it be true that I hear, which is that the Count my husband is far in love with your daughter." To whom the gentlewoman said, "Madam, if the Count love my daughter, I know not, albeit the likelihood is great; but what am I able to do in that which you desire?" "Madam," answered the Countess, "I will tell you, but first I will declare what I mean to do for you if my purpose be brought to effect. I see your fair daughter of good age, ready to marry, but, as I understand, the cause why she is unmarried is the lack of substance to bestow her. Wherefore I purpose for recompense of the pleasure which you shall do for me to give so much ready money to marry her honorably, as you shall think sufficient." The Countess' offer was very well liked of the lady, because she was poor; yet having a noble heart she said unto her, "Madam, tell me wherein I may do you service; and if it be a thing honest, I will gladly perform it, and the same being brought to pass do as it shall please you." Then said the Countess, "I think it requisite that by some one whom you trust you give knowledge to the Count my husband that your daughter is and shall be at his commandment. And to the intent she may be well assured that he loveth her indeed above any other, she must pray him to send her a ring that he weareth upon his finger, which ring as she knoweth he loveth very dearly. And when he sendeth the ring, you shall give it unto me, and afterwards send him word that your daughter is ready to accomplish his pleasure, and then you shall cause him secretly to come hither, and place me by him (instead of your daughter); peradventure God will give me the grace that I may be with child, and so having this ring on my finger and the child in mine arms begotten by him I may recover him, and by your means continue with him as a wife ought to do with her husband." This thing seemed difficult unto the gentlewoman, fearing that there would follow reproach unto her daughter. Notwithstanding, considering what an honest part it were to be a mean that the good lady might recover her husband, and that she might do it for a good purpose, having affiance in her honest affection, not only promised the Countess to bring this to pass but in few days with great subtilty, following the order wherein she was instructed, she had gotten the ring, although it was the Count's ill will, and took order that the Countess instead of her daughter did lie with him. And at the first meeting, so effectuously desired by the Count, God so disposed the matter that the Countess was begotten with child, of two goodly sons, and her delivery chanced at the due time. Whereupon the gentlewoman not only contented the Countess at that time with the company of her husband but at many other times so secretly as it was never known, the Count not thinking that he had lien with his wife, but with her whom he loved, to whom at his uprising in the morning he used many courteous and amiable words and gave divers fair and precious jewels which the Countess kept most carefully; and when she perceived herself with child she determined no more to trouble the gentlewoman but said unto her, "Madam, thanks be to God and you I have the thing that I desire, and even so it is time to recompense your desert, that afterwards I may depart. The gentlewoman said unto her that if she had done any pleasure agreeable to her mind she was right glad thereof, which she did not for hope of reward but because it appertained to her by well doing so to do. Whereunto the Countess said, "Your saying pleaseth me well, and for my part I do not purpose to give unto you the thing you shall demand in reward but for consideration of your well doing, which duty forceth me to do." The gentlewoman then constrained with necessity demanded of her with great bashfulness an hundred pounds to marry her daughter. The Countess perceiving the shamefastness of the gentlewoman, and her courteous demand, gave her five hundred pounds and so many fair and costly jewels as almost amounted to like valor. For which the gentlewoman, more than contented, gave most hearty thanks to the Countess, who departed from the gentlewoman and returned to her lodging. The gentlewoman, to take occasion from the Count of any farther repair or sending to her house, took her daughter with her and went into the country to her friends. The Count Beltramo within few days after, being revoked home to his own house by his subjects (hearing that the Countess was departed from thence), returned. The Countess knowing that her husband was gone from Florence and returned home was very glad, continuing in Florence till the time of her childbed, being brought abed of two sons which were very like unto their father, and caused them carefully to be nursed and brought up, and when she saw time she took her journey (unknown to any) and arrived at Monpellier, and resting herself there for certain days, hearing news of the Count, and where he was, and that upon the day of All Saints he purposed to make a great feast and assembly of ladies and knights, in her pilgrim's weed she repaired thither. And knowing that they were all assembled at the palace of the Count ready to sit down at the table, she passed through the people, without change of apparel, with her two sons in her arms. And when she was come up into the hall, even to the place where the Count sat, falling down prostrate at his feet, weeping, saying unto him, "My lord, I am thy poor infortunate wife, who to th' intent thou mightest return and dwell in thine own house, have been a great while begging about the world. Therefore I now beseech thee, for the honor of God, that thou wilt observe the conditions which the two knights that I sent unto thee did command me to do; for behold, here in mine arms not only one son begotten by thee but twain, and likewise thy ring. It is now time then (if thou keep promise) that I should be received as thy wife." The Count, hearing this, was greatly astoned, and knew the ring and the children also, they were so like him. "But tell me," quoth he, "how is this come to pass?" The Countess, to the great admiration of the Count and of all those that were in presence, rehearsed unto them in order all that which had been done, and the whole discourse thereof. For which cause the Count, knowing the things she had spoken to be true (and perceiving her constant mind and good wit and the two fair young boys to keep his promise made, and to please his subjects and the ladies that made suit unto him to accept her from that time forth as his lawful wife and to honor her), abjected his obstinate rigor, causing her to rise up, and embraced and kissed her, acknowledging her again for his lawful wife. And after he had appareled her according to her estate, to the great pleasure and contentation of those that were there and of all his other friends, not only that day but many others, he kept great cheer, and from that time forth he loved and honored her as his dear spouse and wife.

Commentaries

SAMUEL JOHNSON

from *The Plays of William Shakespeare*

[Note to V.ii.56–57: "though you are a fool and a knave you shall eat"] Parolles has many of the lineaments of Falstaff and seems to be the character which Shakespeare delighted to draw, a fellow that had more wit than virtue. Though justice required that he should be detected and exposed, yet his "vices sit so fit in him" that he is not at last suffered to starve.

[Note to V.iii.21–22: "the first view shall kill/All repetition"] Shakespeare is now hastening to the end of the play, finds his matter sufficient to fill up his remaining scenes, and therefore, as on other such occasions, contracts his dialogue and precipitates his action. Decency required that Bertram's double crime of cruelty and disobedience, joined likewise with some hypocrisy, should raise more resentment; and that though his mother might easily forgive him, his king should more pertinaciously vindicate his own authority and Helen's merit. Of all this Shakespeare could not be ignorant, but Shakespeare wanted to conclude his play.

[General comment] This play has many delightful scenes, though not sufficiently probable, and some happy characters, though not new, nor produced by any deep knowledge of human nature. Parolles is a boaster and a

From *The Plays of William Shakespeare* (1765).

coward, such as has always been the sport of the stage, but perhaps never raised more laughter or contempt than in the hands of Shakespeare.

I cannot reconcile my heart to Bertram; a man noble without generosity, and young without truth; who marries Helen as a coward and leaves her as a profligate; when she is dead by his unkindness, sneaks home to a second marriage, is accused by a woman whom he has wronged, defends himself by falsehood, and is dismissed to happiness.

M. C. BRADBROOK

from *Shakespeare and Elizabethan Poetry*

Hovering uncertainly in date between early and late nineties, *All's Well That Ends Well* is a play which is of its age rather than for all time.[1] It might have as subtitle "Two plays in one," for the reason of its neglect—and the reason why in spite of the title, all did not end well, and it is not a successful play—is that a personal and an impersonal theme are here in conflict. It began by being a "moral play," a grave discussion of the question of what constituted true nobility, and the relation of birth to merit. This was *the* great topic of the courtesy books, and in a court that included such a high proportion of self-made men as Elizabeth's did, the question was not without practical consequences. Such questions were the equivalent of a political discussion today. But in *All's Well* the "social problem"—to give it the modern term—of high birth, exemplified in Bertram, and native merit, exemplified in

From *Shakespeare and Elizabethan Poetry*. London: Chatto & Windus, 1951, pp. 162–170. Reprinted by permission of Chatto & Windus, Ltd.

[1] In the following pages I have summarized my article "Virtue is the true Nobility" *R.E.S.*, N.S., vol. I, 4 (1950). Those who are interested will find there a more extended account of the background of courtesy literature, and in particular the relation of civil nobility to Christian nobility as it is treated by the writers of courtesy books, and books of nobility.

Hellen,[2] is bisected by a human problem of unrequited love. The structural center of the play is the King's speech on nobility, by which he justifies Hellen's marriage: the poetic center is Hellen's confession of her love to the Countess. Few readers would deny that this speech is different in kind from anything else in the play:

> I know I love in vain; strive against hope;
> Yet in this captious and intemable sieve
> I still pour in the waters of my love,
> And lack not to lose still. Thus Indian-like,
> Religious in mine error, I adore
> The sun that looks upon his worshipper
> But knows of him no more.

(1.3.203–09)

This is the voice of Juliet.

> My bounty is as boundless as the sea,
> My love as deep; the more I give to thee
> The more I have, for both are infinite.

(2.2.133–35)

Seen through Hellen's eyes, Bertram is handsome, brave, the glass of fashion and the mold of form; seen through older and wiser eyes, he is a degenerate son, an undutiful subject, a dishonorable seducer. The two images blend in the action as he sinks from irresponsibility to deceit, but makes a name for himself in the wars. He ends in an abject position: no other hero receives the open condemnation that Bertram does. Modern taste may disrelish Claudio, Bassanio or Orsino; but Shakespeare does not ratify it.

---

2 Her name is so spelt throughout the folio text. There is only one occasion on which the meter requires Helena. Shakespeare evidently took great care over his proper names; consider the way in which the diminutives Harry and Kate are used (like Jane Austen, he seems to think only the best people worthy to be called Henry): the beauty of his new forms, Desdemona and Cordelia. James Joyce erected a considerable biographic speculation upon Shakespeare's aversion from the name Richard.

Here all the harsh words are spoken upon the stage: all but Hellen condemn Bertram. After suffering rebukes from his elders, his contemporaries, and even his inferiors, he ends unable to plead any excuses,[3] in danger of the law. The characters of the Countess and Lafeu were invented by Shakespeare, and the King's role much expanded, in order that judgment might be passed on Bertram. By these three, who have an equal share of blood and merit and are therefore impartial judges, he is compared with Hellen throughout the play, to his increasing disadvantage.[4] In the end she alone can restore the honors he has lost.

Bertram is very young, perhaps seventeen or eighteen at most, left without a father's direction and highly conscious of his position. He is handsome, courageous, winning in manners; but also an inveterate liar. Yet the Elizabethan code of honor supposed a gentleman to be absolutely incapable of a lie. To give the lie was the deadliest of insults, not to be wiped out but in blood. Honor was irretrievably lost only by lies or cowardice; a gentleman, as Touchstone remembered, swore by his troth, as a knight by his honor. Crimes of violence were less dishonorable: the convicted liar was finished socially. Bassanio, though he thinks of a lie at the end, to get himself out of an awkward situation, does not utter it.

Bertram's fall is due to ill company: Parolles, or Words, another character of Shakespeare's own invention, is perceived in the end by Bertram himself to be the Lie incarnate, a fact which everyone else has known from the

[3] E.g. 4.2.11–30 where Diana rebukes him: 4.3.1–39 where the young Lords criticize him. Parolles's sonnet to Diana, "Dian, the Count's a fool," contains some nasty hometruths. In the last scene the King and Lafeu are quite uncompromising. Bertram's word is no longer of the slightest value (5.3.182–84).

[4] The Countess is convinced of Hellen's virtue in the first scene (1.1. 40–48), but not so fully of Bertram's. She loves Hellen as her own child (1.3.100–01, 144–46) and after Bertram's flight disclaims him for her son and takes Hellen as her only child (3.2.69–70). Lafeu's view of Bertram is never very high (2.3.100–102). In 4.5. he and the Countess unite in praise of Hellen's memory and at the beginning of 5.3. the king laments her and accuses Bertram's "mad folly" in which he is heartily seconded by Lafeu, who joins his condemnation with still more praise of Hellen.

beginning.[5] He is that principal danger of noble youth, the flatterer and misleader, the base companion against whom all books of behavior issued lengthy warning. The relation of Bertram and Parolles resembles that which every one except Prince Hal takes to exist between himself and Falstaff. Parolles claims to be both courtier and soldier but his courtship is entirely speech, as his soldiership is entirely dress. Even the clown calls him knave and fool to his face; he is ready to play the pander, and at the end he crawls to the protection of old Lafeu, the first to detect and, with provocative insults, to "uncase" him.

The model of a perfect courtier is set before the young man by the King, in a "mirror" or portrait of his father.

His father's "morall parts" are what the king wishes for Bertram; their physical likeness has already been commented on. The elder Rousillon was a soldier first of all, but also a courtier.

> . . . in his youth
> He had the wit, which I can well observe
> To day in our young Lords, but they may iest
> Till their owne scorne returne to them unnoted
> Ere they can hide their levitie in honour:
> So like a Courtier, contempt nor bitternesse
> Were in his pride, or sharpnesse: if they were
> His equall had awakd them, and his honour
> Clocke to it selfe, knew the true minute when
> Exception bid him speake: and at this time
> His tongue obeyd his hand. Who were below him
> He us'd as creatures of another place,
> And bow'd his eminent top to their low ranks. . . .
>
> (1.2.31–43)

Such is Bertram's inheritance of conduct, and he had a duty to live up to it. Hellen's miraculous cure of the king,

---

[5] E.g. the Countess (3.2.90–92), Hellen (1.1.105–7), Parolles is meant to be representative of the evils of the court, which are much stressed in the opening scenes. It is no longer the fount of good manners, exclusively, as it had been in *Two Gentlemen of Verona.*

which is proffered by her and accepted by him and the
court as an act of Heaven,[6] makes her a candidate for
nobility, though she is only the daughter of a poor gentleman belonging to the least dignified of the professions.[7]
The recognized causes for ennobling the simple were
headed by "virtue public," that is, some great public service. Sir Thomas Elyot had declared that nobility is "only
the prayse and surname of virtue" and set forth the eleven
moral virtues as the model for his Governor. Desert for
virtue is Hellen's claim, and this, all but Bertram allow her.

By making his social climber a woman Shakespeare took
a good deal of the sting out of the situation. The question
of blood and descent versus native worth was an ancient
subject of debate on the stage; indeed the first secular play
to survive, *Fulgens and Lucres,* deals with precisely this
matter. Here the lady's verdict was given for the worthy
commoner against the degenerate nobleman. Though noble
descent was prized as giving a disposition to virtue, and
the opportunity of good education and good examples, yet
"one standard commonplace on nobility took shape; that
lineage was not enough, but that the son of a noble house
should increase and not degrade the glory of his ancestors."[8]

Hellen has been conscious throughout of her humble
station, and has urged the Countess that though she loves
Bertram she would not have him till she should deserve

6 The formal couplets in which Hellen, after making ready to retire,
suddenly returns and announces herself as a minister of Heaven mark the
portentousness of the occasion. See Hardin Craig, *Shakespeare's Bad
Poetry* (*Shakespeare Survey,* I; Cambridge, 1948). The automatic writing
down of such passages as "first draft fossils" is not justified. Hellen's
"miracle" is discussed at length by Lafeu (2.3.1–44), it is "a showing
of a heavenly effect in an earthly actor," as Hellen confirms (2.3.65) to
the court.

7 For those younger sons of the nobility who were obliged to take to
the professions, Law was considered the noblest study; the profession of
arms was of course the oldest and most honorable, but it notoriously failed
to supply means of livelihood. The physician was concerned with base
matters, and approximated too nearly to the barber-surgeon and the
apothecary to receive much honor.

8 John E. Mason, *Gentlefolk in the Making* (Philadelphia 1935), p. 8.
This book is the most comprehensive account known to me of the doctrine
of gentility.

him (1.3.201). Before and after marriage she thinks of
Bertram as her "master" as well as her lord, a title Parolles
will not give him. It was within the power of the King to
confer honor where he chose; and Hellen had already been
ennobled in a superior way by being marked out as the
instrument of Heaven towards the King's recovery.

When therefore she is offered her choice of a husband,
none save Bertram think of refusing her. The "lottery" is
like a reversal of Portia's caskets, for here the lady makes
her choice, sure to win. In bestowing a wife upon his ward,
the King was certainly doing no more than Elizabeth or
any other monarch might do. Yet Bertram's cry, "A poor
physician's daughter my wife!" would not sound so outrageous to an Elizabethan ear as it does today, for marriage out of one's degree was a debasing of the blood which
blemished successive generations. The King, in his great
central speech, whose formality is marked by the couplet
form, replies and sets out to Bertram the causes why he
should not disdain merit. This speech contains the germ of
the play—or one of the two plays which together make up
this story.

> Tis only title thou disdainst in her, which
> I can build up: strange is it that our bloods
> Of colour, weight and heat, pour'd all together
> Would quite confound distinction: yet stands off
> In differences so mighty. If she bee
> All that is vertuous (saue what thou dislik'st,
> A poor Phisitians daughter), thou dislikst
> Of vertue for the name: but do not soe:
> From lowest place, whence vertuous things proceed,
> The place is dignified by th' doers' deede.
> Whence great additions, swells, and vertue none,
> It is a dropsied honour. Good alone
> Is good without a name: Vileness is so:
> The propertie, by what it is, should goe,
> Not by the title. She is young, wise, faire,
> In these to Nature shee's immediate heire:
> And these breed honour: that is honour's scorne,
> Which challenges it selfe as honour's borne,

And is not like the sire: Honours thrive
When rather from our acts we them derive
Then our forgoers: the meere words, a slave
Deboshed on every tombe, on every grave:
A lying Trophee, and as oft is dumbe
Where dust, and damn'd oblivion is the Tombe
Of honour'd bones indeed . . .   (2.3.118 ff)

This is doctrine of a kind which ought to convince Bertram. It is only after he has objected, "I cannot love her, nor will strive to do it," that the King exercises his power to compel submission.

The customary formula when presenting young people to each other in such circumstances was, "Can you like of this man?" "Can you like of this maid?"; in other words, can you make a harmonious marriage? Love was not expected. If Bertram is thought to show peculiar delicacy in demanding passion as the basis of marriage, he removes all such notions at the end of the play by his alacrity in accepting Lafeu's daughter, a match which the King had planned since their childhood. In the original story, Beltramo protests his unwillingness but he does not defy the King, nor does he recant as Bertram so abjectly does under the King's threats, protesting that he now sees Hellen to be ennobled by the royal choice. The King's fury, far more reasonable than old Capulet's when Juliet exercises a right of rejection, depends on his and everyone else's conviction that Hellen is "vertuous" and the special favorite of heaven. Not only his king but his mother accepts it. That Bertram should misprize her is not in keeping with the decorum of the play. This is not *Romeo and Juliet;* it is written upon quite different premises, the social premises which that play so pointedly omits. And Bertram has no precontract; for his vamped-up excuse in the fifth act that he was really in love with Mademoiselle Lafeu is patently one of his fibs. He dislikes Hellen on social, not personal grounds. He is being willful; and in running away after the marriage ceremony, he is evading obligations which are imposed by the Church as well as

the State, as Diana does not fail to recall to him (4.2.
12–13).

His rejection of Hellen must be seen then not in isola-
tion but as linked with his choice of Parolles. The first
dialogue of Hellen and Parolles, the Liar and Virtue as
she herself designates them, must be seen as the encounter
of Bertram's good and evil angels, who, if this were a
morality play, would contend for his soul in open debate.[9]

The exposure of Parolles' cowardice and lies precedes
but foreshadows the exposure of Bertram. The last scene,
which is Shakespeare's improvement of his source, is a
"judgment," like those which conclude so many of Chapman's comedies. The most extraordinary stratagems are
practiced by Diana and Hellen to extract Truth from the
Accused. The jewels which are bandied about have symbolic significance; they stand for a contract and an estate
of life. The King's gem derived from him to Hellen, and
Bertram neither knows nor cares what it is. His own
monumental ring symbolizes all he has thrown away.

> an honour longing to our house
> Bequeathed down from manie Ancestors,
> Which were the greatest obloquie i' th' world
> In me to lose   (4.2.42–45)

This jewel, with which he had taunted Hellen, is found
at the end to be in her keeping. Hellen too is a "Jewell"
(5.3.1) which Bertram has thrown away. In this scene
the King appears as the fount of justice, as earlier he had
been the fount of honor; he deprives Bertram of all honor
(5.3.182–84) and the rapidity with which he jumps to
thoughts of murder is prompted as much by his affection for

---

9 Parolles, it should be noted, is a character entirely of Shakespeare's
own invention. His alterations of his source (ultimately Boccaccio, *Il
Decamerone*, 3.9), are highly significant, tending to greater humility, and
dependence on Hellen's part—in the original she has a fortune—and
greater perfidy, weakness and youthfulness on Bertram's. I do not wish to
suggest that *All's Well* is a morality disguised, but it is a moral play, which,
like *The Merchant of Venice*, depends on a central theme of ethical significance.

Hellen as his well-merited distrust of her lord. Lafeu and the Countess also recall Hellen's memory with sorrow. The likeness with the later play of *Measure for Measure*,[10] which was evidently modeled in part on *All's Well*, is particularly strong in this judgment scene, with charge and countercharge piled up in bewildering succession till they are resolved as if by magic in the appearance of the central figure. The ingenuities of Hellen, like those of the Duke, are not to modern taste but their purpose is conversion.

Bertram's conversion must be reckoned among Hellen's miracles. It is notable that on the fulfillment of the bargain she turns to seek, not her husband, but the King. What is achieved is public recognition of her right, which he concedes her. She has been acknowledged by her lord; that her personal happiness is simply irrelevant, and the ending neither hypocritical nor cynical, can be granted only if the play is seen as a moral debate on the subject: Wherein consists true honor and nobility?

This is a grave subject—more lofty than that of *Romeo and Juliet*, for example. But such a subject needed to remain upon the level of debate. An Elizabethan audience might have been quite willing to see it worked out as a species of morality play, without taking the personal aspect into account. What is now called "the love interest" is generally overweighted in the modern view of Shakespearean comedy. His audience would be well accustomed to see a love-intrigue provide the spring of the action without providing any of the interest or body of the play, as it does in the comedies of Jonson or Chapman, where

---

10 *Measure for Measure* has in common the rejection of a devoted bride for insufficiency, and a marriage compelled by the ruler; the substitution of one woman for another; the false self-accusation of the chaste woman followed by denial from the culprit and culminating in his exposure through the arrival of an absent person. The similarity between the themes is also noticeable: both plays deal with what Bacon called "Great Place," the problems of authority, and both are moral plays; that is to say, they are concerned with general truths explicitly handled, though handled in human terms. But *Measure for Measure* seems to me to belong to a much later period; the close resemblances in plot, far from suggesting that the two plays were written close together, imply that Shakespeare returned to his earlier material when he returned to a similar theme.

it is like the love interest in a detective story, strictly sub-ordinate to the disguisings. But here the nature of the story makes it extremely difficult to insulate the marriage as a social and religious contract.

Two incompatible "species" are mingled because the personal aspect awakened to life. The play is a genuine hybrid, one of the few examples of Shakespeare's failure to master and control his form. Bertram is magnificently drawn: his petulance, his weakness, his cublike sulkiness, his crude and youthful pride of rank. His charm has to be accepted because Hellen loves him, but there is little other evidence for it. Hellen's love, as expressed in her three great speeches, is a devotion so absolute that all thought of self is obliterated; yet her action cannot but make her appear, however much more modestly to an Elizabethan than to us, a claimant, and a stickler for her bond.[11] The parallels between her love speeches and the sonnets (especially xxxv, lxvii, lxxxii, lxxxiv, xcv, xcvi), something in common between the lineaments of Bertram and those of Adonis, Bassanio, and Proteus, suggest that the theme of high birth versus native merit, first approached impersonally, had touched off reactions which could not properly be related to the story as it originally stood. The figure of Bertram, so radically changed from that of Boccaccio's Beltramo, is drawn with a fullness, a kind of uncynical disillusion which makes Hellen as a person still more unsatisfactory. She is a voice of despair breaking into the play; at other times a pliant lay figure on which the characters drape their admiration. No crude and direct personal equation can be thought of; Shakespeare would certainly not wish to unlock his heart on the public stage. But here for once the poet and the dramatist are pulling different ways.

---

11 Hellen's three great speeches (1.1.85–111, 1.3.193–219, 3.2.103–34) have a number of parallels with the sonnets. The picture of her as a canny fortune hunter is entirely twentieth-century, and may lead critics so far as to see in her careful disclaimer of any ambition to match with the "royal blood of France" a vulgar foresight, rather than a due sense of rank. Elizabeth's sense of what constituted suitable matches was extremely strict: the Earl of Essex was considered to have committed a shocking impropriety by marrying the widow of Philip Sidney.

He set out to start a discussion on the fashioning of a gentleman and found himself impelled to draw the likeness of one whom Lafeu called an "asse" and Hellen the god of her "idolatrous fancie," but whose portrait stands out clearly as something more complex than either.

RICHARD DAVID

from *Plays Pleasant and Plays Unpleasant*

To the Old Vic goes the credit for the one production
of the season [winter 1953–54] that was full of interest and
excitement throughout—*All's Well That Ends Well*. By
every test it should have been a thoroughly bad one, and I
have heard that a young actor-producer of talent walked
out halfway through the performance declaring that he
had never seen a worse. Faced with a difficult play to put
over, Michael Benthall resorted to all the most disrepu-
table tricks of the trade—drastic cutting, transposing, the
masking of awkward speeches with music or outrageous
buffoonery. Yet it was not only in spite of these tricks but
partly because of them that the producer was able to offer
a coherent, convincing, and, as far as I know, a new
view of Shakespeare's play, at least to those who are prepared to allow that in theatrical affairs the end may justify
the means.

The difficulties of the play are rather conceptual than
verbal. We have had it drummed into us by every com-
mentator that this is a problem play, and that its subject
is "unpleasant"—in Shaw's sense or worse. No modern
audience, we are told, can stomach a hero as priggish and
as caddish as Bertram, or sympathize with a heroine who

From *Shakespeare Survey 8* (1955), edited by Allardyce Nicoll. Reprinted by permission of Cambridge University Press.

like Helena is determined that a man who does not love her shall accept her as his wife, and who resorts to the most ignoble tricks to cheat him into doing so. The comic subplot of the Braggart Parolles is despicable in its barrenness, and the only characters in the play that deserve attention and respect are the King of France and the Countess Rousillon, who both possess a wise nobility worthy of a better play.

Benthall's first step was to take the King and the Countess down a peg. The King became a figure of fun and the affairs of his court pure farce. He was attended by a couple of comic doctors, one fat, one thin, and by a friar who kept up a running Paternoster in a high monotone. His speeches were punctuated by sudden grimaces and yowling cries as his ailment griped him. Even his lucid intervals were diversified by similar "business." During the long speech to Bertram in which the King recalls his youth, the courtiers began to chatter among themselves, growing louder and louder until he was driven to shout them down. When he made a joke he would pause until the court had duly acknowledged it with forced laughter. After his cure at Helena's hands he still remained something of a caricature, with the tetchiness of Old Capulet and the blether of Polonius. The Countess was not ragged to this degree, but Fay Compton played the part not as the aristocratic paragon of tradition but as a very human old woman whose nobility appeared rather in what she did than in the doing of it. She was bent and crabbed, her gestures had an arthritic awkwardness, her utterance was creaky, abrupt, arbitrary. By such treatment both King and Countess became more homely, nearer to earth, and their judgments on the action more humanly convincing from their being more than a little touched with human frailty.

To this roughly individual and "de-idealized" Chorus was added a powerful reinforcement in the shape of Michael Hordern's Parolles, which should have utterly shattered the theory that Shakespeare's Braggart is a more than usually inept version of the dullest of all stock figures. This Parolles was brimful of vitality, and a master-

piece of comic invention. As befits one who is to be found
a sheep in wolf's clothing, he began by looking the oppo-
site, his long hungry face in itself a comic contrast to the
gay Florentine doublet with its huge hanging sleeves. The
wolf soon begins to look a good deal sillier, and Hordern
was brilliant in inventing a series of mimes to express
Parolles's attempts to maintain his dignity in face of Lord
Lafeu's quizzing—hurt, and chilling at the first suspicion,
a scraggy cockerel when trying to outface his tormentor,
at last swallowing with anguish the sour plum of his
inability to answer back without calling down retribution.
His gait was as expressive as his face. His entry in pro-
cession with the victorious Florentine army, himself in
dudgeon over the disgrace of the lost drum, brought down
the house—a jobbling, uncoordinated motion, head
bobbing forward between limp shoulders from which the
arms dangled, feet flapping carelessly down in the abandonment of utter disgust. Equally satisfying was his return,
in apparent eagerness to recapture the drum single-handed,
the beaky nose uplifted and seeming to draw the rigid,
gawky body after it in overacted determination. And in the
climax to this subplot, the interrogation of Parolles by the
practical jokers who have ambushed and blindfolded him,
every move and every tone was deft and delightful: the
anxious gabbling of the numbers as he tumbles over himself to betray the military strength of his own side, the
confidential becking of his interrogator in order to impart
one extra titbit of lying scandal about his superior officers,
the self-hugging satisfaction at getting through the inter-
view, he thinks, so adroitly. When Parolles is finally un-
blindfolded, and discovers his captors to be his own
comrades, Hordern managed an immediate and breath-
taking transition from farce to deadly earnest. At the
discovery he closed his eyes and fell straight backward
into the arms of his attendants; then, as with taunts they
prepare to leave him, he slithered to the ground, becoming wizened and sly on the instant, and with "simply the
thing I am shall make me live" revealed an essential mean-
ness not only in Parolles but in human nature as a whole.
For effect the moment is akin to Lear's "unaccommodated

man is no more but such a poor, bare, forked animal as thou art"; but whereas it is the physical insignificance of man that Poor Tom shows us in a flash, Parolles gives us his spiritual degradation.

Having provided a rough and realistic framework to the drama, the producer could afford to play down the awkward facts of life in its main argument. Accordingly the story of Helena and Bertram was given the remoteness of a fairy tale, or at least of the medieval fabliau from which Shakespeare took it. The sets immediately suggested the sense in which the story was to be read. Behind the three arches of the permanent facade a backcloth with a country scene that might have come from an illuminated manuscript created Rousillon; an equally stylized view of Florence transported us to Italy. When the action shifted to Paris, sliding panels of Notre Dame quickly blotted out the country, while in Florence the undisguised manipulation of hinged screens composed the Capilet interior. Against such ingenious and delicate stage contraptions it was appropriate that Claire Bloom should play Helena as Cinderella. Opinions about this actress differ, and I was prepared to find no more than a beginner of talent whom youth, beauty, and an appearance in a notable film had magnified into a star. I am still in two minds about her. She moved with admirable grace, she had an appealing and ingenuous charm, and—except for a few tiresome mannerisms—she spoke musically and with authority, even managing the awkward couplet soliloquy in her first scene with a skill that made an insult of the instrumental accompaniment officiously provided by the producer. And yet her performance made no coherent impression, and the spectator was left in irritated puzzlement as to what exactly the actress had been driving at. Her vehemence in the early soliloquies—was it impulsiveness and the sudden abandon of passion long pent up? Her almost hysterical reaction when trapped by the Countess into revealing her secret love for Bertram (a scene to which Fay Compton's motherly shrewdness gave a rare tenderness)—was this violence the index of a gentle nature torn between love and loyalty, or of a wayward obstinacy? Did the aggressiveness of her rejoinders to Parolles's innuendos come from the self-confidence of innocence or the hardness of a worldly-wise little bourgeoise? No doubt some of these conundrums are implicit in Shakespeare's lines, but it is the business of the actress to resolve them; and slowly the conviction dawned that Claire Bloom was not even attempting the task, that her emphasis came of nothing more than an eagerness to inject the maximum of feeling into every phrase and word. To be blunt, I think she was ranting—and yet she ranted distinctly, there was music if not meaning in her rant; and again what should have been a blemish turned out to be a positive contribution to the total effect of the play. A fairy-tale princess should not be too closely accountable for her actions, and the wildness of this Helena's regrets, even that trick of making her exit lines trail off on a rising intonation, like a great bird taking wing, gave an other-worldly quality to her story.

Bertram's task was easier. He had only to look like Prince Charming (which John Neville did) and to speak handsomely (which he did also). Such distinction, even unaided, might have overborne all our scruples as to the decency of Bertram's conduct, even to the shameless shifts of excuse to which he betakes himself in the last scene. This Bertram, however, was given every assistance by the producer who, taking a hint from Lafeu's "No, no, no, your son was misled with a snipt-taffeta fellow there," made Parolles responsible for all Rousillon's misbehavior. Bertram, too much a schoolboy still to be allowed by the French King to go to the wars, was shown taking his cue at every step from his unsavory pedagogue. It was Parolles whose nods and becks strengthened Bertram in his first resistance to the King's command that he should marry a commoner. Having married her, he appeared to soften towards her, and would have given her the kiss she so pathetically begs at parting had not a "Psst!" from Parolles recalled him to his previous resolution. Shakespeare makes Parolles the factotum in Bertram's arrangements for the disposal of his wife; Benthall made him the prime mover as well.

King and Countess as Disney dwarfs, the hero and heroine reduced to decorative pasteboard, Parolles taking over the play as a sort of amateurish Mephistopheles— no wonder the orthodox were disapproving. Yet to me at least this lightening and depersonalizing of the story, this removal of the play into the half-world of pantomime and Grimms' Fairy Tales, suddenly revealed its kinship not, as is usually supposed, with *Measure for Measure* and *Troilus,* but with the last romances. With these it shares the theme of paradise lost and paradise regained: the penitent Bertram recovers the wife he has cast off as surely as do Leontes and Posthumus, and his restoration to Helena makes her as much amends as the meeting of Ferdinand and Miranda does to Prospero. Here, however, it is themselves that the losers lose and find, and their redemption is their own and not the work of another more innocent generation. The pattern in this condensed form does not perhaps make so good a play as in its extended shape, where the processes are more clear-cut; but it does make a play, a much better play when seen as a first sketch for *Winter's Tale* than as a botched *Measure*.

Suggested References

The number of possible references is vast and grows alarmingly. (The *Shakespeare Quarterly* devotes a substantial part of one issue each year to a list of the previous year's work, and *Shakespeare Survey*—an annual publication—includes a substantial review of recent scholarship, as well as an occasional essay surveying a few decades of scholarship on a chosen topic.) Though no works are indispensable, those listed below have been found helpful.

1. Shakespeare's Times

Byrne, M. St. Clare. *Elizabethan Life in Town and Country*. Rev. ed. New York: Barnes & Noble, Inc., 1961. Chapters on manners, beliefs, education, etc., with illustrations.

Craig, Hardin. *The Enchanted Glass: the Elizabethan Mind in Literature*. New York and London: Oxford University Press, 1936. The Elizabethan intellectual climate.

Joseph, B. L. *Shakespeare's Eden: The Commonwealth of England 1558–1629*. New York: Barnes & Noble, Inc., 1971. An account of the social, political, economic, and cultural life of England.

Nicoll, Allardyce (ed.). *The Elizabethans*. London: Cambridge University Press, 1957. An anthology of Elizabethan writings, especially valuable for its illustrations from paintings, title pages, etc.

Shakespeare's England. 2 vols. Oxford: The Clarendon Press, 1916. A large collection of scholarly essays on a wide variety of topics (e.g., astrology, costume, gardening, horsemanship), with special attention to Shakespeare's references to these topics.

Tillyard, E. M. W. *The Elizabethan World Picture*. London: Chatto & Windus, 1943; New York: The Macmillan Company, 1944. A brief account of some Elizabethan ideas of the universe.

Wilson, John Dover (ed.). *Life in Shakespeare's England*. 2nd ed. New York: The Macmillan Company, 1913. An anthology of Elizabethan writings on the countryside, superstition, education, the court, etc.

2. Shakespeare

Barnet, Sylvan. *A Short Guide to Shakespeare*. New York: Harcourt Brace Jovanovich, Inc., 1974. An introduction to all of the works and to the traditions behind them.

Bentley, Gerald E. *Shakespeare: A Biographical Handbook*. New Haven, Conn.: Yale University Press, 1961. The facts about Shakespeare, with virtually no conjecture intermingled.

Bradby, Anne (ed.). *Shakespeare Criticism, 1919–1935*. London: Oxford University Press, 1936. A small anthology of excellent essays on the plays.

Bush, Geoffrey Douglas. *Shakespeare and the Natural Condition*. Cambridge, Mass.: Harvard University Press; London: Oxford University Press, 1956. A short, sensitive account of Shakespeare's view of "Nature," touching most of the works.

Chambers, E. K. *William Shakespeare: A Study of Facts and Problems*. 2 vols. London: Oxford University Press, 1930. An invaluable, detailed reference work; not for the casual reader.

Chute, Marchette. *Shakespeare of London*. New York: E. P. Dutton & Co., Inc., 1949. A readable biography fused with portraits of Stratford and London life.

Clemen, Wolfgang H. *The Development of Shakespeare's Imagery*. Cambridge, Mass.: Harvard University Press, 1951. (Originally published in German, 1936.) A temperate account of a subject often abused.

Craig, Hardin. *An Interpretation of Shakespeare*. New York: Citadel Press, 1948. A scholar's book designed for the layman. Comments on all the works.

Dean, Leonard F. (ed.). *Shakespeare: Modern Essays in Criticism*. New York: Oxford University Press, 1957. Mostly mid-twentieth-century critical studies, covering Shakespeare's artistry.

Granville-Barker, Harley. *Prefaces to Shakespeare*. 2 vols. Princeton, N.J.: Princeton University Press, 1946–47. Essays on ten plays by a scholarly man of the theater.

Harbage, Alfred. *As They Liked It*. New York: The Macmillan Company, 1947. A sensitive, long essay on Shakespeare, morality, and the audience's expectations.

————. *William Shakespeare: A Reader's Guide*. New York: Farrar, Straus, 1963. Extensive comments, scene by scene, on fourteen plays.

Ridler, Anne Bradby (ed.). *Shakespeare Criticism, 1935–1960*. New York and London: Oxford University Press, 1963. An excellent continuation of the anthology edited earlier by Miss Bradby (see above).

Schoenbaum, S. *Shakespeare's Lives*. Oxford: Clarendon Press, 1970. A review of the evidence, and an examination of many biographies, including those by Baconians and other heretics.

————. *William Shakespeare: A Compact Documentary Life.* New York: Oxford University Press, 1977. A readable presentation of all that the documents tell us about Shakespeare.

Smith, D. Nichol (ed.). *Shakespeare Criticism.* New York: Oxford University Press, 1916. A selection of criticism from 1623 to 1840, ranging from Ben Jonson to Thomas Carlyle.

Spencer, Theodore. *Shakespeare and the Nature of Man.* New York: The Macmillan Company, 1942. Shakespeare's plays in relation to Elizabethan thought.

Stoll, Elmer Edgar. *Shakespeare and Other Masters.* Cambridge, Mass.: Harvard University Press; London: Oxford University Press, 1940. Essays on tragedy, comedy, and aspects of dramaturgy, with special reference to some of Shakespeare's plays.

Traversi, D. A. *An Approach to Shakespeare.* Rev. ed. New York: Doubleday & Co., Inc., 1956. An analysis of the plays, beginning with words, images, and themes, rather than with characters.

Van Doren, Mark. *Shakespeare.* New York: Henry Holt & Company, Inc., 1939. Brief, perceptive readings of all of the plays.

Whitaker, Virgil K. *Shakespeare's Use of Learning.* San Marino, Calif.: Huntington Library, 1953. A study of the relation of Shakespeare's reading to his development as a dramatist.

3. Shakespeare's Theater

Adams, John Cranford. *The Globe Playhouse.* Rev. ed. New York: Barnes & Noble, Inc., 1961. A detailed conjecture about the physical characteristics of the theater Shakespeare often wrote for.

Beckerman, Bernard. *Shakespeare at the Globe, 1599–1609.* New York: The Macmillan Company, 1962. On the playhouse and on Elizabethan dramaturgy, acting, and staging.

Chambers, E. K. *The Elizabethan Stage.* 4 vols. New York: Oxford University Press, 1923. Reprinted with corrections, 1945. An indispensable reference work on theaters, theatrical companies, and staging at court.

Gurr, Andrew. *The Shakespearean Stage 1574–1642.* Cambridge: Cambridge University Press, 1970. On the acting companies, the actors, the playhouses, the stages, and the audiences.

Harbage, Alfred. *Shakespeare's Audience.* New York: Columbia University Press; London: Oxford University Press, 1941. A study of the size and nature of the theatrical public.

Hodges, C. Walter. *The Globe Restored.* London: Ernest Benn, Ltd., 1953; New York: Coward-McCann, Inc., 1954. A well-illustrated and readable attempt to reconstruct the Globe Theatre.

Kernodle, George R. *From Art to Theatre: Form and Convention in the Renaissance.* Chicago: University of Chicago Press, 1944. Pioneering and stimulating work on the symbolic and cultural meanings of theater construction.

Nagler, A. M. *Shakespeare's Stage.* Tr. by Ralph Manheim. New Haven, Conn.: Yale University Press, 1958. An excellent brief introduction to the physical aspect of the playhouse.

Smith, Irwin. *Shakespeare's Globe Playhouse.* New York: Charles Scribner's Sons, 1957. Chiefly indebted to J. C. Adams' controversial book, with additional material and scale drawings for model-builders.

Venezky, Alice S. *Pageantry on the Shakespearean Stage.* New York: Twayne Publishers, Inc., 1951. An examination of spectacle in Elizabethan drama.

4. Miscellaneous Reference Works

Abbott, E. A. *A Shakespearean Grammar.* New Edition. New York: The Macmillan Company, 1877. An examination of differences between Elizabethan and modern grammar.

Berman, Ronald. *A Reader's Guide to Shakespeare's Plays,* rev. ed. Glenview, Ill.: Scott, Foresman and Company, 1973. A short bibliography of the chief articles and books on each play.

Bullough, Geoffrey. *Narrative and Dramatic Sources of Shakespeare.* 5 vols. Vols. 6 and 7 in preparation. New York: Columbia University Press; London: Routledge & Kegan Paul, Ltd., 1957–. A collection of many of the books Shakespeare drew upon.

Campbell, Oscar James, and Edward G. Quinn. *The Reader's Encyclopedia of Shakespeare.* New York: Thomas Y. Crowell Co., 1966. More than 2,700 entries, from a few sentences to a few pages on everything related to Shakespeare.

Greg, W. W. *The Shakespeare First Folio.* New York and London: Oxford University Press, 1955. A detailed yet readable history of the first collection (1623) of Shakespeare's plays.

Kökeritz, Helge. *Shakespeare's Names.* New Haven, Conn.: Yale University Press, 1959; London: Oxford University Press, 1960. A guide to the pronunciation of some 1,800 names appearing in Shakespeare.

———. *Shakespeare's Pronunciation.* New Haven, Conn.: Yale University Press; London: Oxford University Press, 1953. Contains much information about puns and rhymes.

Linthicum, Marie C. *Costume in the Drama of Shakespeare and His Contemporaries.* New York and London: Oxford University Press, 1936. On the fabrics and dress of the age, and references to them in the plays.

Muir, Kenneth. *Shakespeare's Sources.* London: Methuen & Co., Ltd., 1957. The first volume, on the comedies and tragedies, attempts to ascertain what books were Shakespeare's sources, and what use he made of them.

Onions, C. T. *A Shakespeare Glossary*. London: Oxford University Press, 1911; 2nd ed., rev., with enlarged addenda, 1953. Definitions of words (or senses of words) now obsolete.

Partridge, Eric. *Shakespeare's Bawdy*. Rev. ed. New York: E. P. Dutton & Co., Inc.; London: Routledge & Kegan Paul, Ltd., 1955. A glossary of bawdy words and phrases.

Shakespeare Quarterly. See headnote to Suggested References.

Shakespeare Survey. See headnote to Suggested References.

Smith, Gordon Ross. *A Classified Shakespeare Bibliography 1936–1958*. University Park, Pa.: Pennsylvania State University Press, 1963. A list of some 20,000 items on Shakespeare.

Spevack, Marvin. *The Harvard Concordance to Shakespeare*. Cambridge, Mass.: Harvard University Press, 1973. An index to Shakespeare's words.

Wells, Stanley, ed. *Shakespeare: Select Bibliographies*. London: Oxford University Press, 1973. Seventeen essays surveying scholarship and criticism of Shakespeare's life, work, and theater.

5. All's Well That Ends Well

Arthos, John. *The Art of Shakespeare*. New York: Barnes & Noble, Inc., 1964.

Donaldson, Ian. "*All's Well That Ends Well:* Shakespeare's Play of Endings," Essays in Criticism, 27 (January, 1977), 34–55.

Foakes, R. A. Shakespeare: *The Dark Comedies to the Last Plays*. Charlottesville: The University Press of Virginia, 1971.

Halio, Jay L. "*All's Well That Ends Well*," Shakespeare Quarterly, 15 (1964), 33–43.

Hunter, G. K. (ed.). *The Arden Edition of the Works of William Shakespeare: All's Well That Ends Well*. 3d ed. rev. Cambridge, Mass.: Harvard University Press; London: Methuen & Co., Ltd., 1959.

Knight, G. Wilson. *The Sovereign Flower: On Shakespeare as the Poet of Royalism*. New York: The Macmillan Company; London: Methuen & Co., Ltd., 1958.

Lawrence, William W. *Shakespeare's Problem Comedies*. New York and London: The Macmillan Company, 1931; New York: Frederick Ungar Publishing Co., 1960.

Price, Joseph G. *The Unfortunate Comedy: A Study of All's Well That Ends Well and Its Critics*. Toronto: University of Toronto Press, 1968.

Rossiter, A. P. *Angel with Horns and Other Shakespeare Lectures,* ed. Graham Storey. New York: Theatre Arts Books; London: Longmans, Green, & Co., Ltd., 1961.

Schoff, Francis G. "Claudio, Bertram, and A Note on Interpretation," *Shakespeare Quarterly,* 10 (1959), 11–23.

Smallwood, R. L. "The Design of *All's Well That Ends Well,*" *Shakespeare Survey,* 25 (1972), 45–61.

Stoll, Elmer Edgar. *From Shakespeare to Joyce.* New York: Doubleday & Company, Inc., 1946.

Tillyard, E. M. W. *Shakespeare's Problem Plays.* Toronto: University of Toronto Press, 1949; London: Chatto & Windus, Ltd., 1950.